Praise for Thrifty Witchery

"You will find everything you need to create a powerful witch-craft practice or build upon an established path. Together, Martha and Vincent bring years of lived experiences as Witches, offering foundational principles, practical applica-tion, and cost-effective ways to hone one's craft ... They write with unity and wisdom that will benefit all readers."

—Gwyn, witch, Patheos Pagan writer, and cohost of
    3 Pagans and a Cat podcast

"Vincent and Martha will take you on a journey through the ins and outs of the most important tool in your magickal toolbox: *you.* Weaving a tapestry of intuition, wisdom, and intention, you will come to realize the Clair senses are already yours to develop and true magick costs nothing but your time, focus, and energy."

—Opal Luna, author of *Fiber Magick*

"The true power of witchcraft lies within, not in fancy tools or expensive ingredients. The perfect guide for anyone on a budget, anyone who wants to learn eco-consciousness through re-using and recycling, and anyone who simply wants to learn how to connect to the things that exist in abundance around us already to empower their magic. Creative, crafty, and clever, this book deserves a place on any witch's shelf."

—Morgan Daimler, author of *Fairycraft*

T0008723

"In this fantastic and magical new title, Martha Kirby Capo and Vincent Higginbotham join efforts, knowledge, practice, and their completely different life experiences to give you this complete magical guide where you will rediscover and embrace your magical potential step by step. *Thrifty Witchery* is specially formulated for the urban sorcerer of the modern world."

—Elhoim Leafar, author of *Manifestation Magic*

"Higginbotham and Capo offer readers a delightful look at all the ways in which one can work magic and practice the Craft without spending a fortune. *Thrifty Witchery* is an invaluable guide for the budget and eco-conscious Witch … The authors also masterfully teach readers important lessons on connecting to and utilizing the mystical resources already within oneself."

—Kelden, author of *The Crooked Path* and
The Witches' Sabbath

"I wish I could go back in time and give myself this book. It would have made my life (and my magic) so much easier … You don't need to spend money to practice magic, you don't need fancy tools, and you certainly don't need to make your life look like a slick witchy Instagram account. You just need what you already have: yourself and your considerable magical power. *Thrifty Witchery* will help you tap into that power and wield it masterfully."

—Tess Whitehurst, author of *The Self-Love Superpower*

"*Thrifty Witchery* will take you on the journey of awakening to your own power, harnessing your intuition, and working your magick with easy to find resources that won't break the bank. With everything from urban foraging to divining with tarot, Vincent and Martha provide exercises to ignite your witchcraft and have you put it into practice with ease. A powerful book for anyone regardless of whether they are new or old to the path."
   —Whiskey Stevens, author of *Rise of the Witch*

"Whether you're working on a shoe-string budget or are looking for innovative methods of working magick with what you have lying around, *Thrifty Witchery* has your back. Martha and Vincent cleverly explore methods of creating, finding, upcycling, and crafting magickal tools and ingredients that are accessible to everyone regardless of their financial situations. Full of insight and charm, Martha and Vincent emphasize what truly makes the magick work and where power truly lies in casting spells without hurting your bank account in the process."
   —Mat Auryn, international bestselling author of
   Psychic Witch

Thrifty
Witchery

Thrifty Witchery

Witchery

Magick for the Penny-Pinching Practitioner

Martha
Kirby Capo

Vincent
Higginbotham

Foreword by
Jason Mankey

Llewellyn Publications • Woodbury, Minnesota

FIRST EDITION
First Printing, 2023

Book design by Mandie Brasington
Cover design by Shannon McKuhen
Editing by Laura Kurtz

Llewellyn Publications is a registered trademark of Llewellyn Worldwide Ltd.

Library of Congress Cataloging-in-Publication Data (Pending)
ISBN: 978-0-7387-7052-9

Llewellyn Worldwide Ltd. does not participate in, endorse, or have any authority or responsibility concerning private business transactions between our authors and the public.

All mail addressed to the author is forwarded but the publisher cannot, unless specifically instructed by the author, give out an address or phone number.

Any internet references contained in this work are current at publication time, but the publisher cannot guarantee that a specific location will continue to be maintained. Please refer to the publisher's website for links to authors' websites and other sources.

Llewellyn Publications
A Division of Llewellyn Worldwide Ltd.
2143 Wooddale Drive
Woodbury, MN 55125-2989
www.llewellyn.com

Printed in the United States of America

Forthcoming Books by Martha Kirby Capo
Quantum Physics & Magic

Other Books by Vincent Higginbotham
How Witchcraft Saved My Life

About the Author

Martha Kirby Capo is a Solitary Witch currently working with Brigid, Hekate, Cernunnos, and Pan. She is the page manager of Patheos Pagan's shared blog *The Agora*, where she writes as The Corner Crone. Her Moments for Meditation can be heard on KPPR Pure Pagan Radio and on her YouTube channel.

Martha has been extensively anthologized through Skinner House books and Llewellyn Publications. An award-winning poet and lyricist, she has written for several magazines, including *Witchology* and an issue of *SageWoman*. Martha has been a presenter at Florida Pagan Gathering, Turning the Tide, and Mystic South. She is a member of Covenant of the Goddess and Circle Sanctuary.

© Jessica Gentry

About the Author

Vincent Higgenbotham is the author of *How Witchcraft Saved My Life* and coauthor of *Thrifty Witchery*. Mostly self-taught, Vini is not initiated in any traditional form or witchcraft practice. He follows his gut in all things magic but spends plenty of time researching to be sure his intuition is informed by wisdom before setting his intentions. It is Vini's goal to empower others the way he wishes he had been empowered in his early years. He has a dedicated practice with the goddess Hekate and lives in the South East with his husband, youngest son, and dogs.

Dedicated to all who seek, find, and manifest
the magick within themselves.

Disclaimer

The information in this book is solely for educational and entertainment purposes; the authors and the publisher do not offer it as medical advice. For diagnosis or treatment of any medical condition, readers are advised to consult or seek the services of a competent medical professional.

The authors and the publisher make no representations or warranties of any kind. Neither the authors nor the publisher shall be held liable or responsible to any person or entity with respect to any loss or damages caused, or alleged to have been caused, directly or indirectly, by the information contained herein. Every situation is different, and the advice and strategies contained herein may not be suitable for your situation.

References are provided for informational purposes only and do not constitute endorsement of any websites or other sources. Readers should be aware that the websites listed in this book may change.

In the following pages are recommendations for the use of certain herbs, oils, plants, and ritual items. If you are allergic to any of these items, please refrain from use. Each body reacts differently to herbs, oils, plants, and other items; results may vary from person to person. Please do not ingest any herbs if you are not sure you have identified them correctly. If you are on medication or have health issues, please do not ingest herbs without first consulting a qualified medical practitioner.

Please obey all municipal, county, state, and federal laws when foraging and finding any resources listed within this book.

Contents

Exercises and Practices

EMPOWERMENT EXERCISES

Foreword

One of my first Witchcraft books was a collection of "simple" candle spells. Despite the promise of easy candle-burning rituals on the cover, every spell in that book called for at least four candles, plus a full altar of specific ritual tools and deity statues. To say that I was disappointed with that particular spellbook would be an understatement. At the time, I was a very poor college student, and there simply wasn't enough money in my budget for more than one or two candles per spell, let alone a full altar of expensive and hard-to-find magickal tools.

Most importantly, there was nothing in that spell book about how magick works. A spell is a lot more than lighting a series of candles on a nicely decorated altar. Magick starts within us! You can light as many (or as few) candles as you want, but those candles won't do much but illuminate your ritual space and drip wax on your altar unless you embrace yourself as a magickal being. In a world that actively scoffs at magick and often teaches us to think very little of ourselves, it can be hard to seize and take control of our magickal selves. If you are reading this, you can do it, and this book will help.

When Martha and Vincent asked me to write the foreword to this work, all they really gave me was the title. (I think the email was short and to the point: "The book is called *Thrifty Witchcraft;* Jason, will you write the foreword for it?") Because Martha and Vincent are both brilliant and good people, I readily agreed to write what you are now reading but had no idea at the time what truly awaited me. With a book title like *Thrifty Witchery*, I assumed this volume would just be a collection of easy-to-do spells and practical advice for finding inexpensive magickal items (and yes, you'll find a lot of that in these pages), but there's so much more here. Unlike the candle magick book I read in college, Vini and Martha start their book the right way, by helping us to embrace the magick we all carry within us.

There are hundreds of Witchcraft books published every year now, but very few of them will alter how you look at your craft. This is one of those books with the potential to change how you see the world. Lots of authors over the decades have written about embodying magick, but very few books provide the tools or insights to make that possible for most of us. Whether you are a long-term practitioner or a person new to Witchcraft, Martha and Vini are going to empower you and remind you that for magick to work, you don't need six candles and an extensive collection of magickal bric-a-brac.

But what about those of us who like magickal bric-a-brac? Not surprisingly there's plenty of advice for stocking your magickal cabinets inexpensively, but all of that's partnered with new perspectives and innovative ways of doing things. Until this book, I had never considered dumpster diving or going to a church swap meet to find items for my magickal needs, and now here I am contemplating what pair of jeans I might wear on such an adventure. (Old and beat up jeans for the dumpster diving, probably something a little ragged for the swap meet.)

And it's all an adventure, which is one of the things that makes this book such a breath of fresh air. Instead of boring rote advice about visiting the local second-hand store, Vini and Martha make foraging, finding, and fabricating magickal items an experience. After reading this book, finding the items that will best serve you magickly and not strain the budget will feel like its own sort of spellcraft (all while perhaps recycling something and saving it from a landfill).

There are plenty of exercises and activities in these pages too. The magickal exercises will make you a better witch and help you tap into your psychic potential, and the activities are all thoroughly laid out and easy enough to follow. But maybe the best thing about a lot of the activities is that they will have you looking at your witchcraft in a different way. The broken glass and rusty nails hiding in the corner of your friend's garage? Oh, there's a purpose and a spell for those items! Your perspective on the junk drawer in your home is about to change because of *Thrifty Witchcraft*, I practically guarantee it.

Unlike a lot of books being published today, there's no judgment in these pages. Being an "ethical consumer" has always been a challenge (perhaps now more than ever), and Martha and Vini share how to navigate those challenges, but they don't do it in a way that shames someone for shopping at the Dollar Tree or eating a value meal at a fast-food restaurant. (There's magick in a hot sauce packet—don't let it go to waste!) The world we live in is a complicated place, and it doesn't need to become even more complicated through shaming others for their choices. In some areas, the dollar store and the fast-food joint are the only options around.

One of my mottos in magick and witchcraft is that "there are no absolutes." We all do things a little bit differently because we all come from different life experiences. One of the things that makes this book work so well is that Martha and

Vini come from very different backgrounds and work very different types of magick, but it all comes together so well! While reading, you might be able to glean who did most of the heavy lifting on an exercise or spell, but there's a magickal thread that runs through every page of this book. That thread connects Vini and Martha and connects us all to the magickal current that fuels us as witches and provides meaning to our lives.

Follow the thread and go on the journey—a more fulfilling (and often inexpensive) witchcraft awaits!

—Jason W. Mankey
April 2022

Introduction

This book is the beginning of a new journey for you. In a world that urges us to fear we are missing out and is focused on who has what and is theirs better than mine, we offer the practice of Thrifty Witchery as a path to take back and wield your witch power. Many people new to the craft might believe they need to spend a lot of money on expensive tools, arcane herbs, and exotic oils to be proficient at spellcrafting. In truth, magick does not have to be expensive to be effective, and this book offers a practical, penny-wise roadmap to successful and power-filled spellcasting. Regardless of whether you are starting out on the path of witchcraft or are a seasoned professional in the magickal arts, this is your reminder that the cost of witchcraft is not primarily monetary.

In these pages, you will learn to find the magick within yourself by accessing your intuition, wisdom, and intention. Once you have developed a keen understanding of how these three fundamentals of Thrifty Witchery can be recognized, developed, and honed, we will guide you in using them to forage, find, and fabricate most (if not all) your witchy needs. You will learn that the most powerful tool you will ever have is yourself.

To be fully centered in your personal power, you must commit to an unflinching self-examination of who you are and how you express that essence in the world. We are not talking about the kind of self-examination you might do in the mirror before you head out the door for a meeting or a date. We are talking about taking a hard, no-excuses-asked-or-made, clear-eyed examination of what you believe, why you believe it, and how you manifest those beliefs in your life. We are talking about going deep under the surface of your conscious mind to learn what motivates your decision-making mechanisms and which wounds hidden in the dark forests of your unconscious might need to be brought into the light and addressed. We are talking about learning the unvarnished truth about yourself and learning to love who you are just as you are, warts and all.

Know yourself and own your power. This may sound daunting, and it should because it is. The crooked path is not for everyone, but if you have this book in your hands it is almost a sure thing that you are already a few steps along that path. The deepening of your witchery is a winding journey of self-discovery. Each witch earns their stripes, but none of those stripes are identical. It is your individual human experience that will ignite your unique power. Do not expect others to fully understand the way you do witchcraft, and do not waste your energy comparing yourself to anyone else. You are not required to fit into a specific aesthetic for your witchery to be valid.

Meet Your Guides

Getting to know your guides on this journey and understanding why we wrote this book is important to share before we get started. The Thrifty Witchery magickal system is an amalgamation of wisdom sourced from two individuals who have had radically different life experiences. Martha is full of educated book smarts and has lived a life of privilege while

Vincent was educated on the streets as a high school dropout who only later in life attended college. Yet despite the dynamic differences between us we have been able to discern shared truths, and these truths are the backbone of Thrifty Witchery. We believe we have been able to create a system of spellcraft that can be embraced by anyone and is accessible to everyone.

Vincent's Background

Born into a typical middle class white family, on the outside one could safely assume that I would grow up comfortably with very little want for anything. If you have read my first book, *How Witchcraft Saved My Life: Practical Advice for Transformative Magick*, you will know that this did not end up being the case. While my family could have prepared me for all the success a cis white male could expect, things went completely sideways for me. Blaming anyone but myself for this would be difficult to do, and to be honest, I am thankful every day for the twist my life took.

I have known extreme poverty to the point that "winning" meant obtaining a single cigarette from a stranger. I am not going to rehash everything in my first book, but mentioning my poverty does serve a purpose. It was during those lowest moments that a path of witchcraft emerged before me. I came into my power as a witch while impoverished. At first everything was about personal gain while I slowly learned the principles. And honestly, it should not have been any other way because the main thing I learned during that time was that it does not take money to make magick. One of the first times my magick worked was when I had nothing to work with.

Living with a guy who went to an evangelical church and was trying to convert me to heterosexuality was not fun. Sure he had was a warm place with a real bed to sleep in, but the requirements for staying there were ludicrous: I could not be in the apartment if the guy was not there, a nightly curfew was in place, and owning secular music—that is, anything not by a Christian artist—was completely out of the question. I hid my contraband music in the bookbag that always remained glued to me. One night, I sat outside the apartment for an hour and a half past the curfew waiting for the guy to get home—it all became more of a burden than a benefit for me.

At the time I did not think that what I was doing was magick but in hindsight, it was. Pulling out a pack of cigarettes, crying and miserable, waiting for life to get better, I spit a puddle on the concrete in front of me. Opening the pack, one at a time I started tearing the cigarettes apart, pulling the shredded brown leaves from their paper cylinders. Mixing the tobacco in the spit, imagining a better experience, I pleaded to the God of Abraham to help because that is where I was spiritually at the time. I talked to that god about how the tobacco was my sacrifice and I begged that he get me into a better situation. A week later, I was living with a pastor and his family in a real house where I could come and go as I pleased; they even gave me a vehicle to drive.

All I used was body fluid and cigarettes, which may not seem like a big deal but at the time, cigarettes and spit was all I had. Cigarettes were more precious to me than any other material thing at the time. I placed my will, my intention, into a moment when tobacco and spit were simply stirred together, and I asked for what I wanted while giving everything I had. Even though at the time I was not aware that what I had done was spellcasting, all the ingredients were there and that magick came to fruition.

Partnering with Martha to write this book was born out of my idea that I came from literally nothing. I had to be thrifty to survive. Surviving that poverty gave me the lived experience necessary to say, "magick on a budget works, and by the way here are some ideas on how to pull it off." I am not living in poverty these days, and it feels good to say that. I do not have any issue running out to buy some crystals or candles. It is amazing when I think about where I came from. But if I ever forgot where I used to be, the joy of spending on a statue of Hekate or buying another tarot deck would be lost. My experience becomes pointless if I fail to remember that all I need to create magick is my ingenuity and the intention to call forth what I desire.

Martha's Background

My experience couldn't be more different from Vincent's if it had been scripted by a team of Hollywood writers. I was born into generations of social and financial privilege. My childhood was one of swimming lessons at the local country club, private schools, summer-long away-camps bookended by weeks at our vacation home on the coast, horseback riding lessons, ballroom dancing lessons, and deportment lessons. I was expected to capstone my growing-up years by following in the footsteps of my grandmother and mother, joining social clubs, marrying well, and raising the next generation of a pedigreed, purebred elite class.

I didn't start practicing magick until I was in my thirties, devouring Scott Cunningham's books in my years-long search for a spiritual framework that fit. Too Episcopalian for the Pagans and too Pagan for the Episcopalians, my friends at the time referred to me as an "EpiscoPagan." I eventually found a home in the Unitarian Universalist church which, although not a perfect fit, was not at least as hyper-patriarchal as the faith of my childhood.

Despite how diametrically different our backgrounds are, my first magick spell story shares several elements with Vincent's. A workmate of mine had just gotten married, and with that marriage came the health insurance coverage she had lacked for years. She had been experiencing some inexplicable on-and-off bleeding and a curious pain in her belly for several months; now she could finally afford to see a doctor and have some tests run to see what exactly was wrong with her innards.

It was bladder cancer, with a little side-serving of breast cancer to go along with it.

Devastated, she waded into the complicated process of scheduling a battery of additional tests and screenings. She asked several of us who worked with her to lift her up in prayer and healing. The Episcopalian and Lutheran staff members went right to work. And, in my own way, I did too.

At the next full moon, having anointed and consecrated my focus candle, I cast my circle of salt around my tree stump altar and bent all my will and healing energy toward my friend, gathering my energies into a hot, plasma-like ball. After several minutes, when the energy felt like it was almost too big for me to hold any longer, I shoved what I had gathered away from me. I could feel the heat flying out from my skin like a sirocco, a hot wind whirling and swirling my healing intention toward its recipient.

Several weeks later, my workmate told us all that further testing had revealed … nothing. No cancer anywhere, not in her bladder, not in her breast. She was clear.

Do I think I healed her? I can't definitively say one way or the other. I do know several of us from different faiths had committed to raising healing energy for her. I do know what I felt. And I do know her results.

I worked with nothing more than an old stump I had found and hauled back to my house to use as an altar, a candle dressed with olive oil, some salt, and a mighty intention. Vincent worked with nothing more than his spittle, tobacco, and a mighty intention.

While I've known some lean times after walking away from my upbringing of extraordinary wealth and privilege, I've never been unable to pay my bills, much less wondered where my next meal was coming from or where I would sleep each night. Vincent's background taught him how to make do with very little. My background taught me that inherited money, power, and position are shackles that must be broken if one is to embrace and own one's most authentic self, free and clear.

Coming from money and privilege, spending my formative years in a hierarchical society that esteemed what you represented over who you were and then turning my back on that deeply flawed value system shaped me into the frugal witch I am today. I absolutely and categorically refuse to believe that spending more money means making better magick. I grew up with snobbery and elitism and am here to tell you we damn well do not need that kind of folderol for our magick to be powerfully effective; I will preach that gospel until my dying day, and it is why I have partnered with Vincent to write this book.

What You'll Find in This Book

Magick is already in your metaphysical DNA. In *Thrifty Witchery*, you will learn to tap into your dormant gifts through focusing your intuition, wisdom, and intention. You will learn how to use the energies inherent in all the ways earth, air, fire, water, and spirit manifest themselves. As you develop the intangible gifts you already possess, you will learn how to determine which tools will work best in your practice. You will become adept at seeing magick all around you no matter where you are—in the city, in the countryside, everywhere in between—and you will develop the self-empowerment that is a crucial component of spellcasting and living your best life as a witch.

Whether or not one identifies as a witch, each of us is equally capable of manifesting our will upon the world. Humans have been exerting their will upon the world for eons, but the way witches do this is unique: we align our energies with the unseen energies that are constantly swirling all around us. We do not require anything other than our self-empowerment, intuition, wisdom, intentions, and the drive to manifest what we are endeavoring to achieve to see tangible results.

While altars, ritual gear, tools, and herbs and oils help feed the aesthetic so commonly found in modern social media posts, none of it is necessary. We can effectively practice our craft well outside of the constraints of the so-called must-haves that others have told us are indispensable to powerful spellcrafting. We can forage, find, and fabricate our tools and materials, creating a magickal stockpile that is uniquely tuned to our specific energetic signature.

In the first half of the book, you will learn to access magick from the deepest parts of yourself by tapping into your magickal DNA. We will do a deep dive into the principles and philosophies that underpin the practice of Thrifty Witchery through an in-depth examination of the dynamic energy exchanges between intuition, wisdom, and intention. We will explore how understanding and mindfully developing these foundational skills are crucial components of empowering your magick. The range of topics includes how to recognize and connect with the energetic signatures around you and how to align your energies with those of the elements you have chosen to work with so that your spellcrafting is successful. The book moves from the realm of these critical competencies that are by their nature intangible into the world of the tangible, examining how intuition, wisdom, and intention—in addition to the self-empowerment they feed and develop—undergird the embodied expressions of your magick.

The second half of the book covers the practical skills of foraging, finding, and fabricating the tools, oils, spells, and other accoutrements of your witchy way of life. You will discover that the cost of your magick often is not in terms of the money you spend; instead, the price you pay to do magick in Thrifty Witchery is counted in the currency of your time, effort, and will. You will activate the metaphysical skills you developed in the first half of the book to expand your ability to see and access the magick that is already all around you. You will learn how to recognize the interrelationships between foraging, finding, and fabricating and how these relationships parallel the interrelations of intuition, wisdom, and intention. We will also outline the cross-relationships between each component of the metaphysical and material aspects of Thrifty Witchery.

Throughout the book you will find exercises that are designed to help you apply the practice of Thrifty Witchery to your spellcrafting. In the first half of the book these are called Empowerment exercises. These exercises are designed to help you focus on the more esoteric fundamentals explored in part 1. When you build your intuition, wisdom, and intention you learn to flex different metaphysical muscles. These exercises will help you to increase the strength and flexibility of those muscles.

The second half of the book moves away from exercises and transitions into what we call Practical practices. These are hands-on projects that you can create and imbue with your intentions for pennies on the dollar. Guided by the principles of reusing, recycling, reducing, refurbishing, and repurposing, each activity offers an opportunity to put all of what you have learned in this book together to create magickal tools that are distinctively attuned to how you manifest your will. All the Empowerment exercises and Practical practices are accessible, cost virtually no money, and will help you develop a practice of Thrifty Witchery.

Throughout the book we have tried to be mindful about inclusivity across multiple categories including classism, physical ability, cultural appropriation, and gender. Our goal is to present a magickal system that can open the practice of witchcraft to everyone who wishes to pursue it, regardless of income. We hope to give you the keys to self-empowerment by showing you how to expand your intuition, wisdom, and intention so that you can forage, find, and fabricate any tools your witch's heart may desire.

Magick is already in your metaphysical DNA. Let's get ready to invite it to come out and play.

THE
INTANGIBLES

In Thrifty Witchery are three metaphysical aspects of magick that function as your guides. These are: intuition, wisdom, and intention. When woven together and practiced regularly, this skillset supports and feeds a witch's self-empowerment. In part 1, we explore each of these intangible aspects of magick and how they can be applied in practical and foundational ways to develop a practice that liberates you from the restrictions of feeling like you must own a particular item or tool to create power-filled spells. In the pages that follow we dive deeply into how to identify and apply competencies that already exist inside of you, freeing you to tap into magick that is uniquely yours.

CHAPTER 1

Self-Empowerment

Real-world witches do not look or behave in the ways we see on television, in movies, or in fiction. They do not physically levitate, shoot energy balls at their foes, or magickally control everything in their world. Witches do not always behave or live in the ways we see on social media either. In truth, images and stories on Instagram are often almost as fantastical as the portrayal of witches in most other media. The result is that almost every depiction of a witch or their setup that you ingest on social media seems almost purposefully designed to lead a viewer into the fear of not being witchy enough. While there are some witch influencers on social media who do not have a goal of making others feel as though they are not witching the right way, just as many witch influencers *do* have that goal because they are selling something "guaranteed" to help ease the nagging feeling that you are just not doing witchery right. Either way, these curated images can and often do cause many of us to compare what we do or how we look against what we see depicted. We're here to tell you that you do not have to keep up or compete with any other witch's way of doing anything to be a powerful, power-filled practitioner. You already have everything you need to develop your witchery inside of you.

There is one crucial, must-have component of practicing magick, and it is something that every one of us possesses—ourselves. We are the activator of our own magick. While there are several methods of tapping into the energies around us, the first and most important thing that any witch needs to understand is that we are the power. It is only after embracing the truth that our magickal practice starts and ends with us that we are then able to access and effectively manipulate the energies around us.

Through self-empowerment and an understanding that you are the magick, you are able to grow a formidable practice using only yourself as a tool. Long before any altar or found item can hold power for you, you must first recognize and then cultivate your own strengths from within.

The ability to lead yourself and your magickal workings from a place of intuition, wisdom, and intention can only be achieved after you as a witch acknowledge and accept that you are an empowered being. And, to push the point further, this acknowledgement strengthens your skills in foraging, finding, and fabricating your magickal tools.

And so, the first place to start in using magick is with you, the practitioner.

You Are the Magick

The most powerful magickal tool you will ever own is yourself. This is true whether you are a person of independent means answering to no one or a person dependent on others for your room and board. It is true regardless of age except for the very young, whose cognitive abilities are still developing, and it is true no matter your living situation. Self-efficacy—the confidence that you can control your own behavior, your own motivations—can be attained even in restrictive environments.

Maybe you feel as though you cannot do magick because you live with other people who exert power over you, financial or otherwise. You can still develop self-efficacy. Even if it is not safe for you to come out of the broom closet—and let's face it, there are many places and situations when it is not safe—you can still develop and strengthen your magical DNA. There are witches whose physicality is in some way significantly restricted: witches whose health and well-being are maintained through pharmaceuticals and/or routine therapies, witches who depend on government assistance, and witches who live paycheck to paycheck. And yet, all are powerful practitioners because magick resides within all of us, pure and simple as that. You are not required to possess anything other than your own intentions and the drive to accomplish whatever you are trying to manifest.

The ability to manifest our desires is a skill that all humans have. Whether subconsciously summoning our desires or intentionally walking the path of witchcraft, we all innately possess the ability to bring about physical change through metaphysical means. After all, we manipulate the world all the time to meet our wants and needs.

It is a commonly accepted scientific fact that humans are largely made up of water.[1] The total varies between 50 and 75 percent; however, the fact remains that all of us are at least half or more composed of this liquid building block of life.

....

1 "The Water in You: Water and the Human Body" United States Geological Survey [USGS] Water Science School, May 22, 2019, https://www.usgs.gov/special-topic /water-science-school/science/water-you-water-and-human-body?qt-science _center_objects=0#qt-science_center_objects.

Yet if we were to cut ourselves open, we would not see water even though the science is verifiable and rooted in fact. We know we are made up of water and most of us do not question this; we accept it as fact.

As is the case with water, so too are we all vessels of magick. Some would argue that we are 100 percent magick, citing the autonomic functions that run our bodies without our conscious effort. We are designed—whether by motive force or evolution or a combination of both—to breathe, blink, and pump blood without a thought on the matter. While we now categorize these autonomic and somatic experiences as science, there was a point in human history when we did not know why or how these things happened—they were considered magick. This understanding that, through continued experimentation and exploration, evolved from a magickal categorization to scientific one is one of the reasons we (like so many people) think that in many ways, science can often be simply magick explained.

Whether our journey into manifesting was fueled by an initial understanding of the Law of Attraction (positive energies attract positive energies and likewise for negative energies) or we were introduced to the practice of magick through a Hollywood depiction of witchcraft, we all found our way to this moment of realization: we are magick. Many of us have been informed by the works of Scott Cunningham, Silver RavenWolf, Gerald Gardner, and Aleister Crowley. Others are influenced by more recent teachers such as Thorn Mooney, Heron Michelle, Jason Mankey, Laura Tempest Zakroff, and Devin Hunter. Whether they are old school or new vanguard, each of these teachers agrees on at least this shared truth: magick is in you. The need for tools, altars, herbs, clothing, or anything else can vary according to the teachings of specific lineaged and initiatory covens, but the one thing magick absolutely must have in order to be manifested regardless of the different ways to witch is the witch themselves.

Empowerment Exercise
Knowing You Are Magick

Find a space where you can be alone and undisturbed. It can be a quiet space outdoors, on your porch when everyone is sleeping, or in your room when others you may live with are otherwise occupied. Get into a comfortable position, center yourself, and sink into your body for a moment. Attune to your heartbeat and imagine how it is pushing blood throughout your body. You do not "make" your heart beat; you do nothing to cause the blood to race through your veins and arteries, and yet it does. Your heartbeat is purely autonomic. Acknowledge that you have limited control over this function and recognize that magick has similar properties. Magick is independently active. Magick resides in all things.

Next, take a slow, controlled breath and examine the difference between regulating your breath and all those moments when you breathe without conscious thought. Like your heartbeat and your blood flow, breathing is independently active. And yet you can exert some control when you hold your breath for a few moments before making the choice to inhale or exhale. Respiration works both by choice and autonomically. Take a moment to sink into the knowledge that your magick is exactly like this. Regardless of whether you decide to consciously engage with it, there is magick within you. It is not dependent on religion or tools. Recognize that you have the power to decide to use it and direct it.

Armed with this understanding, consider the times you have manifested your desires when your magick was autonomic like your heartbeat. When in your life did you get what you wanted with no magickal effort on your behalf, and yet it still felt like magick when your desire came to fruition? When your magick was undirected and yet magickal things happened, did those things come about in the most optimal terms?

Now consider your magick in terms of the similarities it has to your breathing. When in your life have you actively chosen to manifest your desires? What happened when you paid attention to manipulating your magick, controlling it much in the same way as you might when consciously regulating your breath? When you used your magick with the same intention as when you choose to take a breath, was it more focused? Did your outcomes align better with your intentions because you made the decision and effort to see your desires come to pass?

Secure in the understanding that your magick is active even when it is at rest, try to put it to use. Decide that you want something easy, such as seeing a specific kind of bird or hearing a certain song. Then activate the magick in you to receive what you want by using your breath. Inhale, hold the breath, and imagine that you are connecting to the well of magick within you. Radiate your desire from deep within to the edges of your body while you hold that breath, allowing it to flow into every fiber of your being. As you release the breath, speak that desire into the world and imagine it leaving your body, saying "I release this desire into the world. I will receive what I have asked for."

When you see that bird or hear that song, or whatever else you have magickally manifested, you will have all the verification you need to know that you are magick.

Born for This

You were born to manifest the magick that resides within you, and there is a plethora of ways to tap into this ability. Some use the Law of Attraction, while others pray for their needs in a petition to the God of Abraham. In the witch community, we employ spells and rituals, and still others of us follow a wandering path that incorporates a wide variety of elements drawn from various religions or practices as we seek to influence the energies of the world around us to meet our wants and needs. These acts of manipulation are what we call magick.

Some witches learn everything they know about magick from a family member. Others spend time reading books and joining classes to hone their skills. Then there are witches like Vincent, who came into their practice in a much less formal manner. Self-taught witches may not be well-read on the subject of witchcraft. They may have only learned a few things through word of mouth. These witches intuit their way through their journey, picking up pieces as they go and ultimately developing a practice that is highly effective and wholly their own.

Whether or not magick has been passed down, regardless of what drew a practitioner to this way of life, all paths that have led you to your magick are valid. Humans keep secrets and we cannot always know the history of every one of our ancestors. It is safe to say that not all hereditary witches know that they have a magickal bloodline. Whether the witch is born into a family of power or is a person who finds magick and infuses it into their family for the first time, as far as we are concerned, both witches are equally valid and equally respected.

Empower Yourself

For many witches, our capabilities spring from knowing that we are able to shape the world around us through our intentions. This is empowering, and this empowerment is within your grasp.

You probably already know the world is filled to the brim with people who are inundated with messages of disempowerment. Perhaps you are one of those people. Martha certainly was. She came of age during *Roe v. Wade* and second-wave feminism, when a woman could not get a credit card in her name, could not serve on a jury, and could not take legal action against sexual harassment in the workplace.

Vincent spent his adolescence believing that he was living in sin for being a gay man. He was beaten up by bullies and debased by those who wanted to see him stripped of the power that his self-knowledge brought him. It was only after acknowledging that these people feared his strength that Vincent was able to grow into his power. While it has only recently become law that he can marry the man he loves, learning that other people do not set the standard for how he lives has allowed him to experience the world without fear.

Regardless of how the world will attempt to disempower you, it cannot do so unless you allow it. It may seem like a hard pill to swallow, especially if you are reading this in a moment or place of defeat. The truth is, though, that your defeats are what empower you. It is in facing your conflicts head-on that you learn how very strong you actually are. When you believe against doubt that you can accomplish something, your empowerment is activated.

EMPOWERMENT EXERCISE
Addressing Disempowerment

This is an exercise you can complete in one sitting or come back to over time as more thoughts come to mind. Using your preferred method—paper and pen or an electronic device—create a document with two columns. Title one column "Empowered" and the other "Disempowered." Think about areas in your life where you are the ultimate authority and note them in the Empowered column. You may find yourself listing things like "I can choose whatever I want to wear" or "I can spend my free time in whatever way I desire." In the Disempowered column, list the parts of your life where you are not the final authority. These entries could be things like "I don't have the power to make my own decisions" or "I cannot have privacy when I want it."

After you have jotted down a few items in each column, look at what you have written. Are there patterns you can discern? What do the things in each column have in common with each other? How are the things in one column different from what is in the other column? Perhaps you feel empowered to accomplish actions that are personal or private, but you feel disempowered when it comes to enacting choices in the community or in public. Ask yourself what would need to happen for you to feel empowered about some of the items on your Disempowered list. Think about those questions over the next several days and add answers below the columns as they percolate up through your subconscious.

The Four Lessons of Empowerment

There are four lessons that anyone can tap into in order to find the power within themselves: To Know, To Will, To Dare, and To Be Silent. Often referred to as the Four Pillars of Magick or the Witch's Pyramid, tapping into these lessons is another preliminary step in embracing the truth that you are the magick.

To Know

Real magick takes a lot of study. Witches ought to be as curious as crows, and like New Caledonian crows, we are often compelled to collect things (in our case, knowledge) to keep in our toolboxes.[2] No matter where we are on the path, no matter our style of witchery, the drive to study and learn as much as we can to deepen our understanding and strengthen our witchcraft is vital to our evolution as a practitioner.

How can you discern if the material you are reading, seeing, and hearing is authentic witchcraft? Do a little research and validate your sources of information.

The Books You Read

You will see some names popping up regularly in the form of older lore from writers such as Gerald Gardner, Raymond Buckland, Margaret Murray, and Starhawk in addition to more recent contributions from writers such as Jason Mankey, Phoenix Lefae, Lilith Dorsey, and Byron Ballard. Read some of the

....

2 Kaeli Swift, "FAQs About Crows," *Corvid Research* (blog), February 12, 2021, https://corvidresearch.blog/faqs-about-crows.

books by authors whose names keep cropping up during your research; see if any of them resonate with you. Check out the bibliographies in the back of books to see what sources authors used as they wrote their own works, and use that list as a springboard to further reading of texts that have already been vetted by those you consider to be authorities.

An excellent rule of thumb is to notice whether authors you are reading have included footnotes. Including citations and sources shows that an author took time to research what they are teaching, that they went a step further to reinforce their facts and theories with verifiable information that backs up what they are writing. Again, if you trust the author, you can usually trust the sources from which they gathered their research.

Social Media

Witches today can and do use technology. Witchy information on social media sites can sometimes be harder to authenticate, but a little time spent sorting the wheat from the chaff will serve you well. Online communities, blogs, and podcasts can often offer solid information and insights.

We have information literally at our fingertips, which means two things: we are inundated with conflicting truths thus leaving it to us to identify what does and does not work for us, and knowledge is abundant and usually inexpensive to access. In this age of information, there is no reason you cannot be learning constantly despite social media being plagued with bad information. It is your responsibility not only to learn but to also verify. The path to self-empowerment does not lie in taking information at face value. Fact-check everything and use multiple sources.

Most of your favorite modern witchcraft authors are already on the popular social media sites. Pay attention to who they support or the sources they suggest for learning; this is a great way to help sift through the fodder that clutters social media. If someone you respect and learn from is giving shout-outs to other content creators, check them out to see if what they're teaching makes sense to you.

Joining social media groups is a fantastic way to dive deeper into your knowledge-gathering of the witching world. Seeking mentors and validating your identity as a witch are both achievable goals in groups on various community-based websites. But again, it is your responsibility to discern whether a group is the right fit for you. There is a plethora of options out there. Some groups are meme-heavy and offer little in the way of education or actual interaction. Others can have stringent guidelines and presumptions and may be fairly rigid in terms of expecting you to fall in line with their specific ideology. Because you are a sovereign human, you have the option to sample as many offerings as you like. To really know where you fit in and what works best for you, you will likely have to taste several flavors before choosing your dessert, so to speak.

Your Teachers

What is another way you can tell if the teacher you follow on social media or read is the real deal? Test out a few of their spells and see if they work. If you do not like something about their spell, by all means change it but be clear on the change you are making and why it works for you (we will dive further into this in chapter 2, on intuition). Construct and then test your own magickal hypotheses and theories, then carefully record the results. As much as and maybe even more than anything else, keeping records and analyzing results will increase your power as a witch.

If you can, consider attending local Pagan events. Pagan Pride Day happens at different times across the world and is a great way to get to know local practitioners. Most events will host well-known teachers, so ask a few who they consider to be wise teachers of the craft. With the exception of brand-new teachers on the scene, most speakers at conventions and gatherings have been invited to speak at previous events, which means they have at least some level credibility within the wider Pagan and witch community.

When choosing your teachers, you want to be sure that they are in alignment with your own thoughts and feelings. In other words, if you know the teacher holds beliefs you strongly disagree with, they are likely not the best teacher for you.

As your powers of discernment increase, you will discover the knowledge you glean from your personal relationship with your deity, source of power, or the energies of the universe will also increase. That said, magick is not just reading, watching, and listening; it is also doing, which brings us to the second component that you as a witch need to embrace in order to manifest the magick already in you: action.

EMPOWERMENT EXERCISE
Build Your Knowledge Base

Take a deep dive into any of the witchy reads you may own. Scan through each book looking for footnotes. Take the time to reread the section those footnotes are found in and then identify whether those sections resonate with you. Make a list of the source material found in the footnotes and then seek out that material for further learning.

If you do not have many other witchcraft books, reach out to friends and on social media and ask for suggested readings or authors to pay attention to. Check out your favorite authors' social media accounts for any teachings they may be offering.

Compile a list of the people you decide you want to learn from and search their websites for a list of events where they will be teaching. If an event is near you and within your budget, make a plan to attend.

Finally, check to see if any of the teachers you are drawn to provide podcasts or have been guests on them. Podcasts are often free, and you can usually incorporate listening to them into your daily practice as they tend to be between thirty minutes to an hour long.

Take the time to grow your knowledge from the people and places you already respect. As you progress, you will likely find additional avenues available for more learning.

To Will

As you increase your understanding of who you are as a witch, you must have the self-confidence to act upon the knowledge you have gathered. Yes, you are a witch if you proclaim it, but without action or the will to practice consistently, you will fail to meet your own expectations. You will be a witch in name only. Magick is not just something you activate when you are ready to cast a spell; witchcraft and magick are a way of life every day of your life.

Magick is a practice. Let's say you have a latent talent at basketball. It is unlikely that you will match or exceed your peers unless you actively practice daily. Sure, you may always hit the basket and three-point shots might be the easiest thing you do all day. But if you are not out there with your team running drills and building your endurance, all the other players who are doing these things will become more adept than you are. The rest of the team and likely the players on all the other teams are willing themselves through action to become better all the time. We as witches are required to do the same. This is not to say that you are in competition with other witches—you are not—only that you must continually practice your magick to become more effective and capable of manifesting your desires.

Willing your practice forward is not just about spells and moonlit rituals. It often more closely resembles a daily practice consisting of gratitude, research, divination, shadow work, interaction with other witches, and accessing your higher self. Obviously, these are not the *only* things that comprise a daily practice. Your daily practice should be tailored to reflect your unique essence. Ultimately it is through your daily practice that you will be able to discern the ways in which you are changing, growing, and developing.

If we are honest with ourselves, all of us have times when we are more of an "armchair Pagan" or witch. Sometimes, no matter how dedicated we are to witchcraft, life gets in the way and one day we may realize that our practice has lapsed. It happens to everyone at some point. Hellenic Revivalist and Hekatean Witch Bekah Evie Bel defines "armchair Paganism" as:

> The type of Paganism where you don't actually do anything within your religion, you just believe in "Pagan" things. You might learn

> about and read about your religion. You prob-
> ably engage in discussions and debates about
> Paganism. But other than that, you don't
> really do much with it. You don't do rituals,
> you don't praise the gods (or equivalent), you
> don't really do anything. Your religion is more
> about belief than about action.[3]

If this has happened to you, do not beat yourself up about it! Ease back into your practice incrementally. Pick one or two simple things to add to your current routine and build from there. This can be as uncomplicated as lighting a tea candle while speaking a short daily intention or pouring a bit of water onto the Earth as an offering at some point during the day. Small, achievable steps will bolster your confidence and give you the best opportunities to feel successful as a magickal practitioner. In the case of magick, practice does not make perfect—practice makes powerful.

Empowerment Exercise
Willing Your Witchcraft Forward

Each morning when you wake up, take five minutes to sit on the edge of your bed. Begin to mentally list the things you are grateful for in your life. If you work with a deity, you can incorporate them into this exercise. Use this time to explore how

....
3 Bekah Evie Bell, "I'm An Armchair Pagan," *HearthWitch Down Under* (blog), May 17, 2017, https://www.patheos.com/blogs/hearthWitchdownunder/2017/05/im-armchair-pagan.html.

your life has changed over time. Bring to mind the ways that you have grown or the difficult things that you have moved past.

Build this daily practice into your routine; once it becomes a habit, try to extend the time you spend giving thanks. If you are strapped for time, you can do this during any of your morning routines. The important thing is to be sure to do it every day. As this practice develops, you will find that you are feeling more empowered in your witchcraft. Ultimately, intentionally acknowledging the gifts magick has provided for you will become an automatic component of your daily life.

To Dare

Magick is not strictly transactional, nor is it straightforward. It is not an exaggeration to say that it takes a daring soul to embark upon a magickal life. While there is an energy exchange, you as the practitioner are working with natural and etheric energies that are potentially volatile and greatly exceed your own. Your will and intention can affect those energies but you will never fully control them, no matter how powerful your magick is. Magick is tricky that way. That is why there is such an emphasis on getting the precise phrasing of your intention exactly right. The old saying from Aesop's Fables holds particularly true regarding magick: Be careful what you wish for, lest it come true.

Your magick has a unique signature, reflective of who you are as a witch. That signature is going to take some time and practice to recognize and understand fully. The process takes a certain amount of daring, for you must be willing to try and fail and try again. Each time you cast a spell and note what works great and what does not quite work the way you intended, you are fine-tuning your magick. And just as you evolve and change throughout your lifetime, so too will your magick.

What about that spell that used to work but does not anymore? Maybe your magickal ability has grown and you need to rework your spells to bring them back into alignment with your expanded skills. As for that tool that does not seem to enhance your focus the way it once did, it could be the same thing. Check in with your skill set; if your power has increased, you may want to tweak your tools a little bit. That said, most magickal tools, particularly ones you feel a strong connection with, will be able to keep pace with your magickal development.

The truth about magick is that it is not always going to work. Your deities will not always show up. You will find that there are times when you cannot raise the energy necessary to complete the spell you are attempting. This is normal. Any practitioner who says otherwise is either a liar or not completely checked into reality.

Magick takes so much work, and that is part of the dare. Once you have obtained knowledge and are willing to put the work in, you are next faced with what to do when you cannot perform. The answer is to keep trying. If you learned to ride a bike as a child, it is likely that you started with training wheels. Eventually those came off and you probably fell off your bike a few times as you learned to balance on two wheels. In fact, you could be a skilled professional bike rider and still have a moment where you crash and burn to such an extent that you cause yourself physical harm. But as most people know, it is not about the fact that you wrecked but rather what you did afterward. If you never dared to get back on that bike, you would not have the opportunity to experience the thrill that perseverance can lead to. Magick is exactly like this.

When a spell fails, there is a reason. If you do not take the time to identify that reason and rectify the disconnect, you won't see your desires come into being. When you dare to keep trying and figuring out what went wrong, you are making a sacrifice. Magick sometimes requires a sacrifice; in this case, it would be your continued effort to learn—to dare—to get it right, no matter how long it takes.

EMPOWERMENT EXERCISE
Daring to Breathe New Life into Your Tools

If you have been working a long time with particular tools and have begun to notice that they do not seem to pack the same magickal punch they used to, reconnecting with them can be a way to ensure that their power and yours continue to align as you both continue to grow. This exercise is as profound as it is simple.

If you plan to reconnect with multiple tools, do so one at a time so that you can bring your directed attention and focused energy to each interaction (in our example, the tool is a wand). Find a quiet, comfortable place and try to work during a time when you will not be distracted. You will also need a piece of paper and a writing implement. Place the tool in front of you and allow it to become the focus of your thoughts. Think about what drew you to it in the first place and write it on your piece of paper. You might write things like, "I liked the material it is made from" or "I liked the way it felt in my hand" or any number of qualities that attracted you. Try to list more than one feature, and be as detailed as possible. Review the list you have made. How many of those qualities still hold true for you today? All of them? Some of them? Of the qualities that no longer hold true, why do you think that is? Write down what you have discerned.

Bring your attention back to the tool and resolve to meet it again as if for the first time, using as many of your senses as you can. Examine it with your eyes closely, noting as many visual details as possible. Close your eyes and touch the tool with your fingers, first sliding your fingertips ever so gently over its surfaces and then holding it and sliding it over your own skin. Keeping your eyes closed, bring the tool up near your ears and slide your fingers over the wand's surface. Notice the sound it makes. Bring the tool to your nose and inhale, staying alert to any scents it has. If you are comfortable doing so—and only if you are sure that the tool's material is non-toxic—gently bring it to your mouth and place the tip of your tongue on its surface. Notice how it tastes.

Finally, cup the tool in your hands, holding it just before your mouth. Open your eyes so that you may gaze upon it as you draw in a deep bellyful of air through your nostrils, hold it for a few seconds, and release it through pursed lips over the tool. Do this at least three times. As you are breathing out your sacred essence, you may want to whisper the following words over it, "I meet you where you are. I invite you to join me on my magickal journey." Hold the tool in your cupped hands over your heart space for a few moments, allowing it to catch the rhythm of your heartbeats before setting it aside and moving to the next tool you plan to reconnect with.

To Keep Silent

The final skill that allows magick to flow through you more freely is knowing when to keep silent. This is about discernment as much as it is about energy exchange. Your magick works because you believe in it. You set your intentions based on your knowledge, you will your desires into being, and you dare to try until you see results. But the whole process can be for nothing if the wrong people provide contrary input.

When you keep things to yourself or only trust a few witches with the details of your practice, you are keeping faith. Magickal power is something that, while accessible to all practitioners, is yours alone. Knowing that you are magick is one thing but reinforcing it with the support of those who believe in what you are doing is a whole new ball game. If you allow others to weigh in on what you are doing and their opinions conflict with your own then you are met with self-doubt, and often this is what can cause your magick to fail.

Maintaining an air of secrecy is vital for your witchy practice if you intend to fully tap into your own personal power. Because the magick is in you, it is only you who can identify what works and does not work in your practice. When you invite others into your magickal bubble, you are not only inviting them but also their personal notions of how magick works based on the magick that is in them. We are individuals and as such, magick does not work the same for everyone. Therefore, we suggest you adapt spells and identify the tools or principles that work best for you knowing that the particulars of each person's magickal practice will be unique to them. Magick is not one-size-fits-all. It cannot be. We are far too unique, and expecting that the manner in which one of us performs a spell is the one and only way it should be done by everyone is ridiculous.

In fact, anyone who *does* believe this should be avoided when it comes to sharing magickal efforts—they are not going to be a good influence on your practice.

EMPOWERMENT EXERCISE
Silence Makes Your Magick Stronger

Look through your spellbook or, better yet, the spells in some of the witchy reads you may own. If you do not own any witchy books, search the internet for a spell that may help you with something in your life. Once you find one, deconstruct it: take each component of the spell apart and examine what it calls for or what it requires from you. List the components of the spell that work for you, discard those that do not, and rebuild the spell in your own image.

Next, attempt the spell on your terms with your adaptations. How did the spell feel? Did it work for you? Were there some parts of the spell that rang truer to your particular style of witchcraft than others?

With the data you collect from casting this spell, examine and review the outcome. Decide if the spell can be perfected further. Would it work better as it was originally written? Or would some additional tweaks to the spell help it to resonate with you and your magick better?

Incorporate any additional tweaks and try the spell again. What worked? What did not? Again, spend time with the outcome and decide if the spell can use more fine-tuning.

Repeat this exercise until the original spell has been perfected into a final form that fully aligns with you. Do not seek outside help or counsel—trust only yourself as you silently develop your own adaptations to the magick you are seeking to manifest. Eventually, as you adapt the spell and shape it to fit your needs and your magick, you will find that only you can accurately identify what will work for you. Once you find your strength in silence, you will be able to move forward in casting spells that garner the best results for your wants and needs.

Reconnecting to the Power Within

You maintain a daily practice. It is full of habits and routines that keep you connected to your witchcraft. You maintain boundaries with your practice, such as not worrying about it on the weekends. Anyone who knows you knows you are a witch because you do not have to live in the closet. At work, they ask you to pull tarot on your lunch break and the results are always spot-on. But what nobody knows is that sometimes you think that at some point, everyone is going to find out you are a fraud.

In the echo chamber of your head, it does not matter how many spells have been successful. "You clearly lucked out," whispers your Shadow, "your practice isn't enough. Why aren't you spending the whole day casting spells and making magick candles? Never mind work or all the other distractions. Real-life daily tasks shouldn't matter! You should do witchy stuff all the time!" Maybe you think you do not look the part, so how can you possibly be a "real" witch? And now because of the way you feel, your magick is suffering.

This is an example of imposter syndrome. It happens when, no matter how successful or invested a person is, they believe that at any moment the world will realize they are not all they present themselves to be, or perhaps they decide they have been fooling themselves all along. This is a very real experience, and many witches go through bouts of it. Deep down under all the unnecessary self-doubt, you still know the truth: you are a witch. But when your Shadow starts its seductive whisper campaign against you, it is so easy to succumb to its wily negativity.

Feeling like an imposter is hard. It creates a fissure in your faith and can get in the way of everything you do. While artists, writers, musicians, lawyers, doctors, managers, students, and everyone else can experience this phenomenon, imposter syndrome can be particularly detrimental for a witch. Your power resides within your belief that you can effectively perform magick you have set out to do. When your Shadow tests own certainty, your self-confidence and thus the power of your intention falters. You strip yourself of your own power and in doing so create a self-fulfilling prophecy. The Shadow wins.

Combating this state of mind can sometimes be the greatest challenge a witch can face on their journey. When this feeling is coupled with the perceived faults of not having tools, an altar, ingredients for a spell, or even a cohesive aesthetic, imposter syndrome can often seem like the truth. After all, if you were a real witch, wouldn't you have all those things? Wouldn't people know it just by looking at you? Life is difficult when you lack things—transportation, a job, food, housing, and so on. But a lack that seems to directly affect your spiritual practice can quickly become psychically oppressive, which is another reason we have set out to write this book. We want you to know that you are not alone. You are a witch. Your power exists *independently* of your haves and have-nots.

The first and most important step to take when combating imposter syndrome is to reaffirm your identity to yourself. Remember that you are a witch because you have declared it as your truth. Remember that you make the rules of your magick, and no one gets to define you—you define yourself. Then remind yourself of all you have already accomplished, the magick that you have already cast.

In the end, you are only an imposter if you are legitimately faking the entire experience, and let's face it, faking it is not what witchcraft is all about. You are a witch because that is what you were born to be. You have an infinitely abundant source of magick inside of you. When you accept that fact, you begin to trigger a change in yourself that will allow true magick to flow more freely in everything you do. Using your power means that you will have to learn to control it, bend it to your will, and access it through different practices. One of the ways in which you can tune in to your own energy and the energies around you is through grounding.

Grounding

Grounding is a critical component of successful spellcasting, and it costs absolutely no money. Why is grounding so important? Self-empowerment is all about finding, recognizing, and manipulating your own energies so that you can successfully organize and use them in combination with the other highly active and volatile energies swirling around you, thereby manifesting the results you are seeking in your spellcraft. Before you start to tap into these energetic resources you need to have a firm and clear understanding of who you are as an energetic being. Remember, you are not controlling the energies around you, you are adjusting your highest self to align with these energies and then adding your own energetic DNA to the mix. Grounding yourself deeply into who you are as a witch keeps you from getting lost in a vast energetic sea.

There are as many ways to ground as there are witches. Eventually you will discover what works best for you but for now, let's start with something as common as dirt, something you can think of as starting literally at the ground level. One of the simplest and most effective ways to ground is to place your bare skin against the earth. Your mindfulness is the key to turning this deceptively simple action into a practice that connects you deeply with the earth, yourself, and the energetic exchange that happens when you are intentionally communing with the planet.

EMPOWERMENT EXERCISE
The Practice of Grounding

To build your grounding practice, start by choosing your setting. Again, your choices are wide open here; maybe you have a favorite natural area you visit or a particular place on your property that you are especially fond of. Maybe there is a potted plant in your home that always gives you a little burst of joy when you see it. Think about where you feel most connected to and grateful for our planet. We use the word "dirt" as a catch-all; do keep in mind that the type of earth you may best connect with may not be soil. Earth's crust is a multi-faceted garment that includes not only dirt but sand, clay, rock, shells, marl, limestone, and countless other sediments and minerals.

Next, think about how you want to connect your skin to the earth. Some practitioners gravitate toward bare feet, others find they prefer to sink their hands into the dirt. You may want to lie down upon the earth, allowing for as much skin-to-planet contact as possible. You may want to make mud pies or finger-paint mud swirls onto your skin. As you think about these things—the setting and the particulars of your interaction—you will discern how much privacy you will need.

When you are ready to ground, whether it is in your house next to a potted plant set by a window or a favorite spot in your yard, on a sandy beach or in a nearby nature preserve, get into the position you have determined will be most comfortable for you: sitting, standing, reclining or some combination of those. If you are inside using a potted plant, rest as much of your dominant hand as there is room for on top of the soil.

Breathe naturally as you begin to relax the muscles of your body; you are transitioning into a state of active rest. Notice what is going on around you. If there is a breeze, how are the plants responding to its invitation to play? Are there butterflies or other small creatures? Birds? Spiderwebs? Frogs? Seagulls? Pick one thing to focus on for a little while as you attune your senses to be fully present in these moments. You may notice your eyelids drifting down, or you may notice your focus shifting to something that catches your attention as it moves across your vision. There is no "should" or "should not" in this part of the grounding exercise; release any expectations and continue to relax and sink into what is right here, right now.

When you feel like you have caught the rhythms around you, take three slow bellyfuls of breath, inhaling through your nose and exhaling through your slightly pursed lips, making a gift of the energies you carry deep inside of you. As you inhale and exhale begin to concentrate on the parts of your body that are in direct contact with the earth. Imagine that those parts are becoming heavier while remaining in place, resting against the ground. As they become heavier, they become more and more filled with your attention, your energy. Try to hold this sense of deep connection for at least a few minutes. Imagine that you are gently pushing your energy in rhythmic pulses through that connection and down into the earth.

When you are ready, imagine the parts of your body in direct contact with the earth becoming lighter, less full of your directed energy. Rest gently as long as you need to. Come back into yourself and begin to notice the activities around you again. If you feel like it, be a little playful with the earth, drawing simple shapes on its surface, or scooping up a handful to drizzle across your skin, or poking a finger down into it—whatever feels right and authentic to you.

Before you leave, remember to thank the earth for sharing this energetic exchange with you. Perhaps you will draw the words "thank you" onto the ground, or maybe you will pour a little water onto the ground while whispering or saying the words. Your mindfulness and sincerity make your gratitude a precious gift from your heart.

Once you have determined the where and the how, it is time to think about when you will exercise grounding. Attuning to your own energy and the energies around you very often means finding a quiet time and space where the distractions of your daily life are significantly muted. This often can seem like an insurmountable obstacle for those who have far too many responsibilities and vanishingly small amounts of time to attend to those responsibilities. Your initial efforts will take a little longer than you might expect because the first few times you practice grounding, you are going to want to try to give yourself more than a few minutes to refocus, settle, and attune. Later, as your grounding exercise becomes more routine, you will find you may not need as much time to reach a focused state of attunement.

If it seems like too much to try carving out a quiet time and space in your over-packed schedule, it may be time to show yourself and your priorities a little tough love. Grounding strengthens and refreshes your connection to your magickal DNA. Your energy is a precious resource and the foundation of your witch's power—you need to take care of it. Remember that self-care is not selfish; you are important enough to put your energetic self at the top of your priority list.

Finding Your Magick

When all is said and done, only you can identify and define your magick. You are on a lifelong journey. You are not going to know everything after reading one book or fully fine-tune your will after casting one spell. Even after you dare to persevere a few times and keep silent about the mechanics of your magick, you will always be on a dynamic journey. You are going to hit bumps in the road, run up against blockages and steep inclines, and approach blind curves. Embrace all of it; it is what will lead you forward and help you find your own personal style of magick.

The crooked path is just that: crooked. It is not until you fully understand how magick works that you will be able to break out of the "should" frame of thinking and wholly embrace the "could" approach. So, find your focus objects, learn all that you can, practice until you cannot stand it and then practice some more. Fail, do this a million times, learn from your mistakes, and then keep making new ones. Witches grow. You will change and your practice will develop out of that. Find your people, the ones who believe in you, who practice like you do. Do all this and eventually you will see what you have become. You will look within and see the witch you believed yourself to be, and you will find that the magick is right where we say it is: in you.

CHAPTER 2
Intuition

Empowerment is fed by three metaphysical components, one of which is intuition. A witch's intuition is a potent aspect of their magick. Knowing what to use and how to use it is essentially derived from our intuition and backed up by experimentation and testing of the results. When we pay attention to our higher selves, empowered by the bone-deep understanding that magick resides within us, we begin to open new pathways in our manifestation techniques. Our personal truths and our responses to the world give us insight into how we may best bring our magick into being. Each of us has our magickal "sweet spot" and often we have more than one. This will not be the same for everyone, nor should it be. Your sweet spot is the result of your magickal algorithm and is perfectly aligned with who you are as a witch.

Learning to listen to your higher self is essential in witchcraft. No matter what path you walk, no matter what course of action you are led to take, it is through intuition that you find your way there. Intuition is your direct line to the Source and all its infinite knowledge. Before acquiring wisdom and setting intentions, you must be able to clearly hear what the universe is communicating to you and then act accordingly on that communication.

How do you intuitively access the information all around you? By paying attention. We are all gifted with at least some form of "clair" sense; learning to use yours is one of the best ways to hear, see, know, taste, smell, or feel what the Source is telling you.

Developing and strengthening your intuitive skills is also crucial to accessing the knowledge available through divination. Divination is tapping into divine knowledge to understand a situation. Any form of divination, from reading cards to tea leaves to casting lots, can afford a witch the insight to make sense of information that may at first seem obscure. Paying attention to your dreams or where you travel when your mind wanders is another way of connecting your physical existence to your intuitive journey.

Maybe you have experienced a particular sensation when something has resonated with you, an identifiable feeling in that moment when you suddenly know at a deep, almost instinctual level that something is either especially true for you or has a uniquely personal relationship or correspondence with you. Your intuition is the conduit for that connection.

The examples cited above are just a few of the many ways we use our intuition as witches. In developing and trusting our intuition we strengthen our connection to forms of energy that are greater than ourselves, and we are released from the rigid parameters of logic and reason. It is in this intuitive awareness that we are afforded the opportunity to try something new, something different, to follow our heart, gut, or mind into a more magickal existence. It is through our intuition that we are first introduced to the magick living within us. Intuition leads us forward into understanding the wisdom we gain over time and informs the intentions we set. It is in following our intuition that our journey into Thrifty Witchery truly begins.

What Is Intuition?

Functional intuition requires a conviction that we are being led by something bigger than ourselves. In the big picture, we are only a pixel on the jumbo screen that is the universe. We receive information and project it outward to manifest our desires. When a witch ignores their intuition, they are not only doing a disservice to themselves but also doing a disservice to the source that can inform their power.

In her book *Intuitive Witchcraft*, Eclectic Witch Astrea Taylor defines intuition as "a spiritual lifestyle that celebrates the truth of who we are and what we feel."[4] Elsewhere in the book she writes, "[intuition] tells us what we really want and how we feel about things," an accurate description of what intuition is and how it functions in magick.[5]

We are all driven by our feelings every day. From following a morning wake-up routine to creating a formidable magickal practice, it is our intuition that is at the baseline of the decisions we will make. The routes we take to work and the outfits we finally decide on are all informed by our intuition. When we speak to people and get the good vibes or the bad ones, these nonverbal messages are the result of our intuition receiving information about who those people are, often before we may know them very well.

Intuition is more complex than a simple face-value judgement. It is more akin to assessments based on intangibles, an energetic, emotional, physical, or vibrational understanding of your interaction with the object you are intuiting about. The moments when you focus your mind on how you feel about

....

4 Astrea Taylor, *Intuitive Witchcraft: How to Use Intuition to Elevate Your Craft* (Woodbury, MN: Llewellyn Worldwide, 2020) 2.

5 Ibid., 8.

something offer you opportunities to begin to recognize and strengthen your unique magickal signature.

Our intuition communicates to us in myriad ways. It is likely that no two people truly experience their intuition in the same way. While there are some basic methods by which we interact with our intuition, the larger, more dynamic points of contact with intuition are rather intricate. When tapping into the divine information that is your intuition, it is vital that you first learn which points of access work best for you.

Clair Sensing

Probably the most basic and completely accessible of all the intuitive points of contact are your clair senses. Clair senses are something that everyone has. While there is a vast range of proficiency in using our gifts of clair sensing, we all have at least a minimal ability to access this extra-sensory ability. Often, we have already been experiencing moments when our clair senses are activated without realizing it. We have all had an experience when we just know something, when we can completely visualize a future event. We have all had a gut feeling or heard an answer to our question when no one is talking. Some of us may have smelled a scent that triggers an understanding while no one else can smell it. Others of us may have gotten a literal bad taste in our mouths about a situation even though we have not eaten or had anything to drink in some time. These experiences are your clair senses giving you information and insight.

Developing your clair sense is a way to develop your intuition, as the knowledge is accessed by simply listening to your senses and acting on the information you are receiving from the source. Wisdom bestowed upon you via your intuition is divine, and not all that dissimilar from the ancient oracles' experiences of having visions or listening for messages from the sounds of acorns as they fell. In fact, it is exactly this type of intuition that is fueled by your clair senses.

Clair senses are connected to our five physical senses: sight, scent, taste, touch, and hearing. Many people feel as though we all have a sixth sense, and while the sixth sense they are talking about is technically one of our clair senses, the fact remains that a majority of people do not fully know how to engage in this sixth sense. The sixth clair sense is the sense of knowing. All six senses have their own clair name: clairvoyance, clairsentience, clairaudience, clairgustance, clairalience, and claircognizance.

Empowerment Exercise
Identifying How Intuition Informs You

Consider for a moment a time when you knew your intuition was telling you something. How did that information come through? Was it in a sense of knowing? Did you hear a voice in your mind that was not quite your own? Maybe you had a vision of what was to come before it happened. These are just a few ways that our intuition can inform us.

Learning to pay attention to your intuition requires you to first understand how your intuitive messages present themselves. In this exercise you will spend some time over a few days paying attention to your senses. As you go about your regular daily routines, check in a few times with what your senses might tell you about whatever or whoever it is you are interacting with. For example, if you are taking your lunch in a cafeteria, cue into your senses during that experience. What do they tell you about what is going on around you? What is the general feel of the place, the people, a particular person? What conclusions can you come to without physically interacting with anyone? How did you come to those conclusions?

Identify any moments when you feel, think, know, hear, see, or even taste or smell something that could be an intuitive message, information that you might have no reasonable way of knowing. Once you have identified how your intuition is informing you, use the exercises that follow to enhance your connection to your particular intuitive sense. Note that you may find that your intuition comes through more than one sense.

Clairvoyance

Probably the most well-known of all the clair senses, clairvoyance is the gift of seeing what is happening either remotely in real time or seeing an event before it has taken place. For many people, it is also connected to seeing the spirit world. Clairvoyance is connected to our sense of sight and is one of the most easily accessed clair senses in terms of intuition, as many times people can experience predictive dreams or receive visions that indicate what will soon take place. While these visions may not always be clear indicators of *exactly* what will happen, they do tend to make perfect sense once the event has transpired.

Honing this skill requires practice and a lot of patience. People with strong visualization skills are typically prone to being gifted with this form of clair sense. Be aware that this is not something that everyone can do. Aphantasia, or the inability to see images in your mind, is a very real condition and if you find that visualizing is something you cannot do simply accept that and focus instead on developing the other clair senses.

To develop your clairvoyance, try holding an object in your hands that you are familiar with. Close your eyes and picture it in your mind. As you do this, see every detail and paint an imaginary picture of that object in your mind. Open your eyes, look at the object, and see if there are any details you missed. Try again with a different object. When you have mastered visualizing well-known objects, try the exercise with an object you may not be as familiar with. When you are ready for something more complex, try the following exercise.

EMPOWERMENT EXERCISE
Visualizing What Is Already There

Sit in a quiet place in your house in a room you know well, one that you could walk through with your eyes closed or in the dark. Close your eyes and start to call to mind everything in the room. Picture each item as fully as you can. Spend time on the details. This could mean that you visualize the way a blanket feels or the comfort of the couch you are sitting on. Take time to see the objects of the room. Imagine the colors and textures of everything.

Begin to mentally map out the room in as much detail as you can. Imagine yourself getting up and touching the coffee table or picking up the remote to your television. See in your mind's eye everything that might be hanging on the walls or any décor that might be in the room. Visualize yourself moving about the room and feel the weight and density of a particular item as you pick it up and hold it in your hands.

This exercise may be difficult at first. If you cannot visualize anything, that is okay. Try to build up to seeing the entire scene by starting with just one quadrant of the room. Work with that visualization until you have cemented it, then add another section of the room and so on until you can see the entire room in your mind's eye. Repeat this exercise every day until the details are so vivid that you feel as though you are actually moving about the room even when you physically are not.

Practicing this form of visualization will help you to access your clair sense of seeing and will eventually open you up to being more receptive in those moments when your intuition is communicating with you through clairvoyance.

Clairsentience

Clairsentience is something almost everyone has probably experienced at one time or another. This clair sense is directly connected to our tactility. Our sense of touch is one of the most tangible mundane senses we have, and clairsentience is just as powerful only typically on a more internal, intangible level. When we have a gut feeling that something is not right, this is clairsentience. We may not always know exactly why we have a sudden pit in our stomach, but we do know that our intuition is communicating through our ability to feel in these moments.

With this form of intuition, a witch allows their gut feelings to lead them. Those feelings are informing them about a potential outcome, and very often that outcome ends up being exactly what they thought might happen.

Empowerment Exercise
What Could Have Been

To strengthen this skill, you need to pay attention to what your body is trying to tell you. If you feel as though things are not right or feel compelled to do something, follow that instinct. Over time and with practice, the messages that your intuition offers you through clairsentience become easier to access and following your feelings will become second nature.

The next time you have a gut feeling that you should take a different route to work or that you need to pay particular attention to someone's actions, follow your gut. Let your intuition lead you exactly where it wants to. But don't let this exercise end there. Find out what may have happened if you had not followed your intuition's lead. This might look like checking the traffic report for the road you chose not to travel or keeping tabs on the person you felt like you needed to be careful with after the specific instance has passed.

Evaluate the accuracy of your gut instinct. Was it spot on? Mostly accurate? Way off-base? If it was flat-out wrong, examine what else might have been in play that you may have misinterpreted, and use that new insight to further hone your clairsentience skills. Find out why you were led to do whatever it was that your intuition guided you to and use the answers to keep building your knowledge base.

Clairaudience

Those of us who have functional hearing know that sometimes auditory stimulation can be as big a burden as it is a pleasure.

Music is enjoyable but it can quickly become painfully annoying when it is turned up way too loud. The gift of clairaudience can be just as conflicted. This clair sense is connected to our ability to hear. It manifests in us when we hear something that others cannot. Often a clairaudient might hear their name spoken or a phrase that makes sense only to them, offering insight into a situation they are close to.

Not everybody enjoys hearing what others cannot. It is not unusual to wonder if you are losing your mind when you hear a voice that no one else does. As well, these messages are not always a disembodied voice. Sometimes a conversation you pick up from passersby or a line in a random song on the radio can contain the information you are meant to be hearing.

Strengthening this gift can take practice, but you can learn to understand the messages you are receiving from your intuition when it communicates through clairaudience and incorporate this skill in your divinations.

Empowerment Exercise
Seek Out the Message

To develop your clairaudience skills, try sitting in a place and listening to the sounds around you, not simply hearing them but really listening to them. Learn to pay attention to the nuances of what you hear. You can become aware of and identify sounds that trigger a unique knowing or response in you, and through this awareness your clairaudience will become an increasingly dependable skill. One way to do this is to go to a crowded place such as a shopping mall, a city corner, or even a coffee shop. Without eavesdropping, listen to all that is happening around you. Are there conversations going on, songs playing, or a particular rhythm playing out from nearby construction? Submerge your sense of hearing into everything. If a car drives past with a song playing, pay attention to the line you pick up as it passes. When people having a conversation walk by, notice if a particular phrase or word pops out at you.

Do not interact with the environment beyond simply listening. When your hearing is fully submerged in your surroundings, think of a question you would like to ask. This could be something spiritual or a decision you are seeking guidance on, or it could be as mundane as asking where you might choose to eat dinner that night. With that question in mind, listen to your surroundings more deeply not just with your ears but with your intuition activated. You may hear someone talking about the restaurant they work in; this could be your answer on where to eat or it could simply be random noise. How can you know the difference?

Be aware that the very first thing you hear after asking your question may not be a message uniquely designed for you. Keep listening even after you think you have heard what you think might be the answer. See if you get the same answer from another source of noise in your environment. If you hear the message repeated, then it is probably a true intuitive message. If it is not repeated it is probably just random noise, much like the static you hear when you are dialing a radio tuner trying to find a particular station.

Once you feel you have received and verified your message, be sure to follow through on the answer you intuited.

Take note of what happens when you follow your intuition's advice. What ended up making sense? What didn't? Why? Be aware that you will make mistakes in learning to use and respond to your clairaudience and do not expect results the first few times you work this intuitive muscle out. Remember that the purpose of exercise is to grow and build strength and suppleness, and that by repeating the exercise the skills will eventually become yours to command.

Clairgustance

One of the most recognized diversities in humans lies in our sense of taste. Some love spicy foods while others abhor them. One person may have a sweet tooth whereas another prefers savory bites. Our sense of taste, when practiced mindfully, can be harnessed as a divinatory experience known as clairgustance. This might be where the term, "it left a bad taste in my mouth" originates from at least in some small part.

This gift might be the oddest of all the clair senses, but it is fueled by your intuition, nonetheless. Paying attention to what you taste when you are around people can give you insight into conditions like illness or negativity.

Empowerment Exercise
Tastes of the World

It is possible to strengthen this skill by exercising your palate. To do this, make it a point to begin tasting all sorts of edible items. Acidic foods, spices, bland concoctions, and sweets will all help you to explore the world of taste. For example, knowing the sensation that bitter or sour foods create on your tongue will help you recognize what your intuition is telling you. If you happen to be around a person who feels this way toward you and you realize you have that taste in your mouth even though you have not eaten or had anything to drink, that may be your intuition offering you some additional insight.

As you explore the tastes of the world you will develop a more nuanced understanding of the emotions and feelings that different flavors activate in you. If, for example, you are with a person you don't know very well and get the sense that you have eaten a sweet or begin to crave sweetness it can be your intuition's signal that you can feel pleasure in getting to know the person just as you do when tasting your favorite sweet treat. Conversely, if there is a particular flavor you strongly dislike and you begin to taste that on your tongue when interacting with a person it could be an indicator that you may not want to pursue a relationship with them.

Knowing your preferences and having a dynamic sense of your own palate can sometimes turn eating into a divinatory experience. You may be indulging in your favorite meal and yet for some reason the meal is lacking in some way. The dish has been prepared properly with fresh ingredients, but those flavors you always love just aren't doing it for you. This could be your intuition letting you know that something in your environment is amiss. Paying attention to how your taste has changed during a particular situation can bring you a fuller understanding of your surroundings and possibly open you up to a message about something you once loved.

Ultimately only you can discern what the tastes you experience mean. If clairgustance is an intuition access point you would like to develop, dive in with an open mind and explore as much as you can about the feelings you associate with different tastes. Be sure to keep track of your associations and note any changes you experience over time.

Clairalience

Scents offer a range of experiences from the offensive to the pleasant. A rotten egg may turn your stomach when its sulfurous smell fills the air, while the scent of flowers in full bloom can often lighten your mood. In the middle of this spectrum fall things like gasoline or bleach; some people may love the smell of one or both while others are sickened by them. Our olfactory sense is as personalized as our fingerprints, and the ability to employ clairalience can be a useful addition to your divinatory practices.

Clairalience can range from phantom smells to actual scents that affect you differently than they do others. The smell of food cooking on a stove may seem beguiling to everyone present but, even if you normally enjoy the meal being cooked, in a particular instance you might find that you are put off by it. This can be an indicator that the person making the food has ill will toward you or others present, or it could mean that the person doing the cooking has an ailment that has not yet come to light. Only the individual experiencing this phenomenon can discern the message they receive. To understand these messages, you must begin to pay attention to both what is happening in and how you respond to your environment.

Empowerment Exercise
Keep Track of Random Scents

It is not uncommon to move through the day and catch a whiff of a scent that seems out of place. We are bombarded with scents all the time that originate from very real and mundane sources. But occasionally you may smell something that no one else around you does. In these moments, your intuition could be alerting you to pay special attention to what is happening around you.

When you smell something, say something. This is the key component to this exercise. If others around you smell the same thing you do, that is an indicator that this scent is a mundane experience, and you can move forward without delving into any messages from your intuition. But, for example, if you smell something burning and no one else does, this may be an indication that your intuition is very much in communication with you.

As is the case with all the clair senses, no one can tell you what that burning scent means to you. That meaning is as uniquely yours to discern as the path you walk in life. Our goal here is to simply make you aware that your intuition is communicating with you in ways that you may have been dismissing as fluky or inconsequential. Growing your awareness is the first step to noticing, identifying, then harnessing the intuitive messages you are already receiving.

When you smell something especially when no one else does, pay attention to the feelings the scent evokes in you. Does it make you feel uncomfortable? Worried? Curious? Does it remind you of another time when you smelled the same scent? If so, what was going on and what were your feelings that other time you smelled it? The feeling that corresponds to that scent is the takeaway message for you. The smell of something burning might cause one person to recall when a loved one's home was in flames, while another person might be reminded of a peaceful camping trip. The first person could be triggered into fear while the second person might find themselves remembering a loved one. Your own personal discernments and experiences will be absolutely unique to you.

By now, you will not be surprised to learn that strengthening this clair sense (as with all clair senses) will take time. Once you have learned how to discern whether clairalience has been activated, make notes on what you are smelling, why it is significant at that moment, and what you think the intuitive message is. Later, if or when something comes to light regarding the situation, you will be able to put the pieces together. Through practice, attention to details, and logging your observations you will soon be able to depend on your sense of smell to not only navigate the world around you but to also understand the information your higher self is sending you.

Claircognizance

Of all the clair senses this may be the hardest to discern but is also the most magickal. Claircognizance is the ability to simply know something as if you are pulling information out of thin air. Unlike clairsentience, this is not a clair sense that is aligned with your sense of touch. In fact, claircognizance is typically not connected to any of your five physical senses, although you may often become alerted to it through any one of those senses. You might suddenly have the answer to a question while feeling a chill run up your spine or know that a person is lying to you while hearing a ringing in your ear. To be clear, chills up one's spine and ringing in the ear could be perfectly mundane responses to many things, but when coupled with a sudden knowing, these reactions can often be the result of claircognizance.

Using this sense can be tricky because it often requires that you trust yourself and the thoughts you have beyond what you or others may deem reasonable. Claircognizance is often accompanied by some other form of clair sense as well. For example, while reading your tarot or oracle cards you discern a message from a card that is nothing like the card's well-known interpretation. You are certain that the card's commonly accepted message is not the correct interpretation in this particular case and go with your insight. Or perhaps a sudden and complete knowing washes over you while scrying. In both scenarios, there is a good chance your claircognizance has been activated by your intuition. Claircognizance can also further inform the information you have gleaned from any of the other clair senses.

Empowerment Exercise
Know You Are Knowing

To know something means that you have no doubt about the information that you possess, which can be difficult in a world full of conflicting and changing information. When you experience a sense of knowing, you must have confidence in your claircognizance. That confidence may be difficult for those who often second-guess the information they receive, and it is particularly difficult when what is intuitively known does not seem to align with any previous knowledge.

Still, to build this gift into the strongest possible form of clair sense you must learn to have perfect faith and trust in yourself and your intuition. One way that you can develop this trust is to start small.

When a random thought pops in your head, jot it down. This could be anything from, "I am receiving a promotion today," to "a green car is about to pass me." While these thoughts may come to you in moments when you cannot safely write them down, it really does help to do so. If you can, keep a pad of sticky notes nearby. If an incidental thought suddenly makes itself known, make a note and then wait to see whether that thought comes to fruition.

We all have millions of thoughts all day long, so the likelihood that every single unrelated thought you have will come to pass is not very high. However, through this exercise you will be able to form a hypothesis from which you can identify which thoughts are intuitive claircognizance. These messages could be coupled with a secondary clair sense or may even feel like a sense of knowing that is unique from all the other random thoughts that you have. The process of sorting through what differentiates claircognizance from other passing thoughts will help you to gain confidence in discerning when your intuition has been activated.

When a random thought comes to fruition, keep the sticky note. If that random thought ends up being just one of several amorphous thoughts swimming around in your brain, toss the note.

On the notes that you keep, list what made this thought different from the others. What did you feel that made you think this might be your intuition reaching out? Develop a system of markings to indicate when a thought was aligned with your clair sense of knowing. As you go through your day continue taking these tiny notes and mark them if those previous indicators are present.

As you begin to collect more data on your thoughts and continue to differentiate their qualities, you will begin to become familiar with what your claircognizance feels like. Examine your notes for patterns and discern any consistencies. This is a practical way for you to develop that trust in yourself.

Strengthening your claircognizance requires confidence not only in yourself but also the unseen Source of the message. When you suddenly know something, it is easy to pass the experience off as being overly optimistic or pessimistic. It is easy to assume that you are making things up or fantasizing. The trick is not to be too quick to convince yourself that your moments of instant and complete knowing are valueless. When you begin to listen to the ideas you have and trust the things you know for no discernable reason, you will begin to see that your knowings are derived from spiritual or higher knowledge. Claircognizance is the purest form of intuition. When you begin to trust it, all your divination practices will improve.

Divination

Divination is the art of centering and opening your intuition so that you can discern possible insights about potential outcomes. In play during this centering is a push-pull tension of both/and that is almost (but not quite) a juxtaposition of being in a state of passive readiness to receive insights while at the same time actively seeking to make meaning from those insights.

Predicting future events has been one of humankind's desires since the dawn of history. Take, for instance, the Oracle of Delphi in ancient Greece, the most famous of whom was the Pythia. In the eight century BCE, the priestess became an important consultant in a role that continued to be relevant until the fourth century CE.[6] While there were some men who served as oracles (Aelius Aristides, Oracle of Asclepios in Epidaurus), the vast majority of oracles were women.[7] For more than a thousand years in the ancient world, kings and noblemen sought the advice of wise women on what the future might hold were they to ride into battle or sign a treaty. The role of oracle was one of the very few roles that empowered women in an otherwise patriarchal setting.

It should come as no surprise that today the idea of figuring out what the future holds for any of us is still popular. People all over the world check their daily horoscopes. In the late 1960s through the 1970s, the practices of astrology were in one of their heydays. Mainstream magazines such as *Cosmopolitan* included horoscopes (and still do so), and psychics like Walter Mercado were part of the daily lives of countless people.

People still refer to the prophecies of American psychic Silvia Brown and French astrologer Nostradamus to glean information when disaster strikes. It is not uncommon to hear on the news or read in an article that this prophet or that psychic

....

6 Michael Scott, *Delphi: A History of the Center of the Ancient World* (Princeton University Press, 2014), 30.

7 Alexandra L. George, "Oracles/Sibyls," King's College Oxford Department of Women's History, December 18, 2005, https://departments.kings.edu/womens _history/ancoracles.html.

predicted some tragedy (after it occurs), and many of us in the witching community are eager to develop our psychic skills.

There is a wide range of methods and tools for divination, from tea leaves to tarot cards to pendulums, from scrying (looking into reflective or other surfaces) with smoke or water or mirrors to active dreaming. In short, divination—particularly because so many of the methods require little or no financial outlay—is a penny-wise practice that the empowered witch can embrace and should spend some time developing. Honing your divination skills will sharpen your overall effectiveness as a witch. Why? Because the more aware you are of your own insights and deep knowings, the more powerful your spellwork will be.

The breadth of the many divination practices for understanding your higher self and the world around you are too broad to cover for the purposes of this book. In the chapter on fabricating, we will talk more about some of the divination forms that you can create using the materials you have foraged and found.

Scrying

For the frugal witch, scrying is one of the most economical methods of intuitive divination there is. While most often scrying involves sight, do not forget you can scry through sound as well. For example, in ancient Dodona (once almost as famous as Delphi), the priestesses listened to the wind sighing through the sacred grove and the rhythmic patterns made as acorns fell from oaks into large bronze cauldrons set beneath them. From these sounds they made their prophecies.[8]

....

8 "Dodona," Ancient-Greece.org, August 6, 2020, https://ancient-greece.org/history/dodona.html.

Mention the word "scrying" these days and the first thing that comes to mind for most people is a black mirror or crystal ball; however, you can scry with all kinds of surfaces, including fire. The dynamism of the flames and the added sensory inputs of heat, scent, and sound can add context to what you see in the fire. The combination of these sensory stimuli can facilitate a semi-trance state very easily, and in that state, you can fire-scry the patterns that emerge.

Other people find smoke-scrying to be an effective method of divination. The smoke can be from any source, not necessarily a campfire. In the same way that a fire can be a single flame, the sinuous smoke that curls up from a snuffed candle can be alive with meaning and insight when the practitioner is in a state of relaxed awareness and alert to their intuition.

Water is another element used in scrying. This method most often involves pouring an amount of clean water into a bowl, allowing it to become still, and gazing into its surface with softened eyes and sharpened senses. Another water-based method is creek-scrying. Like fire-scrying, creek-scrying involves several different dynamic sensory stimuli that combine and recombine in recognizable patterns once you have immersed yourself in their rhythms. Cloud-scrying is another water- and nature-based divination practice.

Scrying is a useful tool in the frugal witch's toolkit, so do not be afraid to experiment with different objects in the search for what works best for you and your intuition. Most scrying objects are either free or cost mere pennies. In scrying as with so much of witchcraft, the real expense is energetic; your energy is the precious commodity that you choose to spend when strengthening and working with your magickal intuition.

Seeking Advice from Cards

For many witches, there are countless moments in their practice when they seek advice or guidance. From discerning the potential outcome of a spell to identifying whether a spell should even be cast, witches tend to want to know; most commonly, the divinatory method of choice is tarot or oracle cards. This is not to say that all witches partake of tarot or oracle card divination, but it is safe to say that most turn to the cards at least occasionally to access their intuition and gain insight into their magick.

Like every other tool a witch uses, tarot and oracle cards are a way for the practitioner to focus their energies and activate their deep intuition, even though the cards are not magick in and of themselves, and meanings vary according to several factors surrounding the reading. Just like a wand or crystal or cauldron, tarot and oracle cards offer a type of anchoring and jumping-off point from which the practitioner can allow the wings of their intuition to unfurl and fly.

Tarot

Tarot cards have been around since at least the fifteenth century, but it was not until somewhere in the eighteenth century that they began to be used in the practice of divination. This became known as cartomancy.

In "Tarot is Trending, and Dior Predicted This Months Ago," journalist Breena Kerr writes: "Tarot-deck sales in general are up 30 percent this year [2017], after rising 30 percent in 2016—the highest in 50 years, according to Lynn Araujo, the editorial and communications director for U.S. Games

Systems."[9] Over the last ten years or so, decks have become less patriarchal, less white, and less binary, and modern interpretations are expanding and flourishing.[10] Crowdfunding platforms have also served to help diversify tarot decks, and it only makes sense that as more and more people can see themselves represented in the cards, more and more personalized decks are being created and made available to the public.

Tarot decks can be found almost anywhere. From big box bookstores to small metaphysical shops to Amazon, it is not hard to find a deck that resonates with you. The price range of these decks varies greatly as well. Some higher-end decks are printed on excellent card stock and are sturdy enough to last for some time, and you can sometimes find some lower priced cards that are also printed on the same high quality of card stock. Conversely, it would not be unusual to find an expensive set of cards that, while they are beautifully produced, might lack the sturdiness necessary to stand up to daily usage. In truth, the cost of a tarot deck is not an indication of its quality, and neither is the fanciness of the imagery featured in the cards. In the chapter on fabricating, you will find a Practical practice to create your own tarot or oracle deck that can be just as powerful as any you might purchase from a vendor.

One more note about using tarot cards in divination: most modern tarot readers understand that the tarot does not give you highly defined or rigid outcomes; rather, the themes that present themselves through divination represent energies

....

9   Breena Kerr, "Tarot is Trending, and Dior Predicted This Months Ago" *New York Times*, October 25, 2017, https://www.nytimes.com/2017/10/25/style/tarot-cards-dior.html.

10 Victoria Woodcock, "Why Tarot is Trending Again," *The Financial Times*, April 16, 2021, https://www.ft.com/content/c4afbc05-a715-4b83-9323-44e4c4f95ca5.

around the seeker's question. The cards do not map out an inescapable future. We all have free will and the ability to make choices. The choices we make are part of what maps out our future. Tarot is a method of accessing the subconscious or intuition to glean information pertaining to the concern so that we can make the most informed decisions possible.

"What about Yes/No questions?" you may ask, "those are well-defined answers, aren't they?" But are they, really? It depends. As Benebell Wen writes in her masterwork, *Holistic Tarot: An Integrative Approach to Using Tarot for Personal Growth*, "[The one card] interpretation depends on what question was asked and how the question was phrased, and of course on what card was drawn."[11]

Effective decisions are not made in a vacuum—we live in the world, and the ways of the world affect our decision-making process. Therefore, everything is part of a vast energy exchange; that you are even asking a question (yes/no or otherwise) is the result of some set of prior events or relationships, and the way in which you choose to respond to those events or relationships upon reading the card will affect the nuances of that energy exchange.

Oracle Cards

Oracle cards are another form of cartomancy. While most Rider-Waite-Smith–based decks have a standard seventy-eight cards comprising the major arcana and the minor arcana (four suits with court cards), oracle decks do not have a standard number of cards, do not feature arcana, and are not arranged

....
11 Benebell Wen, *Holistic Tarot: An Integrative Approach to Using Tarot for Personal Growth* (Berkeley, CA: North Atlantic Books, 2015), 284.

by suits. Due to their freer form, many practitioners find oracle cards much easier to read.

As of this writing, the oldest oracle deck is believed to be Hooper's Conversational Cards, published in England in 1775. While not quite as old as tarot cards, oracle cards have certainly been around for a good long while.[12] Oracle cards are created and structured according to their creator's will. They can feature just about anything—fairies, animals, angels, trees, insects, nebulae—there really is no limit to what can serve as the basis of the design system. Some oracle decks feature a single word, phrase, or a few sentences accompanying the image on the card; other times, there is nothing but the image.

Oracle decks tend to speak in the language of overarching themes, whereas tarot decks tend to speak in relatively more specific terms. During a reading many practitioners will employ a combination of oracle cards and tarot cards, drawing an oracle card before a tarot reading to discern what the theme of the reading might be, then drawing the tarot cards to fill in the details of that theme, and finally drawing another oracle card for any secondary themes pertaining to the reading.

Intuition in Our Dreams

Many years ago, in the wee hours of the night long before she identified as a witch, Martha discovered herself floating a couple of feet from the bedroom ceiling. It scared her silly the first few times this happened, particularly because she would wake up to feel the bed bouncing under her as if she had just landed on it. But after it had been happening for a while, she

....

12 Robert M. Place, "A History of Oracle Cards," *Tarot & Divination Decks with Robert Place* (blog), October 25, 2015, https://robertmplacetarot.com/2015/10/25 /a-history-of-oracle-cards.

decided to do a little exploring. She remembers using her fingertips to skim across the ceiling in little pushes that sent her gently sailing through the darkness into the hallway and other rooms of the house. Eventually (and mostly because the sensation of falling was so disconcerting), she made a conscious decision to stop dream flying.

Active or lucid dreaming can be one of the most vital and powerful expressions of intuition a witch can experience, and the good news is that there is absolutely no financial cost involved. It may surprise you to learn that about 55 percent of the population has experienced a lucid dream at least once in their lifetime while about 23 percent of people have lucid dreams at least once a month.[13]

All of us go through Rapid Eye Movement (REM) and non-REM stages during sleep. During the REM stages of sleep, our brains are very active and our heartbeat rate increases as do our eye movements. Lucid dreams usually happen during REM stage sleep.[14] Given that active dreaming is a fairly common occurrence and we all enter the REM stage of sleep, it makes sense that witches who choose to develop this subconscious and deeply intuitive state can turn their dreams into a powerful tool for divination.

Neuroscientists do not know exactly why some of us have lucid dreams, but they do have some ideas based on research. One physical difference that has been discovered between those who have lucid dreams and those who do not is that the

....

13 David T. Saunders, Chris A. Roe, Graham Smith, Helen Clegg, "Lucid dreaming incidence: A quality effects meta-analysis of 50 years of research" *Consciousness and Cognition* 43, (July 2016): 197–215, https://doi.org/10.1016/j.concog.2016.06.002.

14 Kirsten Nunez, Elaine K. Nuo, "Lucid Dreaming: Controlling the Storyline of Your Dreams," Healthline.com, June 17, 2019, https://www.healthline.com/health/what-is-lucid-dreaming/.

prefrontal cortex of those who have lucid dreams tends to be larger than that of those who do not have them. The notion is that people who tend to be self-reflective have a tendency to experience lucid dreams.[15]

So much of Thrifty Witchery is grounded in digging deep to uncover who you truly are at your core and being intentional about how you express that identity authentically. Said another way, at the core of Thrifty Witchery is rigorous self-reflection. You are already developing self-reflection skills as you absorb and perform the lessons presented in this book. Intuition can and does speak to us through our dreams. When intuition reaches out to us in this form, we often do not have to work too hard to figure out the message, and your ability to have and direct a lucid dream can help you decipher what your intuition is telling you.

Sometimes what you see while dreaming does not make sense until several days after you have connected with your intuition in this way. As an example, one night Martha's lucid dream revealed a huge clowder of black cats overrunning a cemetery full of chest tombs, obelisk monuments, raised ledger monuments and headstones. Since most of Martha's lucid dreams involve static objects, she knew that this particular dream, with its high activity level, was unusually important but she was unable to contextualize what she had seen. A day or two later, the US Capitol, a place full of obelisks, monuments, and memorial statues, was overrun by insurrectionists.

....

15 Benjamin Baird, Anna Castelnovo, Olivia Gosseries, and Giulio Tononi. "Frequent lucid dreaming associated with increased functional connectivity between frontopolar cortex and temporoparietal association areas" nature.com, *Sci Rep* 8, 17798 (2018). https://doi.org/10.1038/s41598-018-36190-w.

Empowerment Exercise
Developing Your Ability to Have Lucid Dreams

Lucid dreaming happens during the in-between state when you are not fully asleep nor fully awake. To increase your chances of having a lucid dream, try forming a specific question you would like to gain some intuitive insight about as you are falling asleep. As you become sleepier and your mind begins to drift, do not be overly concerned if the question loses focus; simply come back to it now and again as your mind and body edge toward sleep. The goal is not to keep yourself alert by drilling the question incessantly but to gently bring the question along with you as you begin to fall asleep.

On your way to falling completely asleep, softly focus your eyes to see the backs of your eyelids and notice the colors and any shapes that may form as they shift and swirl. If you find your eyelids drift to become half-opened, do not pay attention to it. Keep your focus on the colors and shapes. Many times, you will discover that these amorphous blobs of color resolve into a scene that unfolds before you. Watch the scene as it comes into focus and note everything about it, including the dominant color. Allow yourself to fall fully asleep. You can also do this exercise before fully waking up. In either case, try not to make any judgements about what you are seeing behind your eyelids; simply observe.

Whether you do this exercise before sleeping or just before you fully awaken, ask yourself some questions about what you saw once you are fully awake. For instance, what was the weirdest thing you saw? Did anything look familiar? What do you think was happening in the scene? If there were people in the scene, did any notice you? Did you interact with anyone in the scene? Write down your impressions, then choose one or two to think about as you go about your daily activities. Notice if there is an intuitive connection between the question you had asked and the scene that unfolded. If so, what might your intuition have been telling you?

There Is a Style for Everyone

Our inner guidance system shapes the efficacy of our magickal practice. For example, some witches resonate most strongly with healing. Working primarily in healing modalities does not make them less of a witch; it simply means that of all the different kinds of magick they create, magick aligned with healing is their wheelhouse. At the time this book is being written, it is popular to bash the "love and light" witches, or whom Marion Weinstein defined as "Positive Witches."[16] This is a bias, pure and simple. We are not created to be cookie-cutter copies of each other. It is our intuition, unique and wholly our own, that helps us discern which components will become the building blocks of our practice.

Vincent prefers to use bay leaves nearly every time he casts a spell. This is because culturally this herb resonates for him and has been a mainstay in his life since he was a small child. When his intuition tells him that a bay leaf is necessary for the magick he is performing, he does not question it. Often the herb might not even correspond with the goal he has set out

....

16 Marion Weinstein, *Personal Magic: A Modern-Day Book of Shadows for Positive Witches* (Newburyport, MA: Red Wheel/Weiser, 2021), 8.

to accomplish, but he finds a way to align his intention with his intuition regardless.

The truth is that our intuition will lead us in diverse and unique directions. It would not be unusual for one witch to resonate with a specific correspondence in their magick that another witch cannot even wrap their mind around using for that particular spell. Not only is every witch unique, so is every human being in addition to the way we become strongly attuned to our specific surroundings and environments.

Resonance, the sparking of your intuition, is all about that feeling of rightness when something is presented to you. A message in a movie can resonate with you just as much as a tarot card reading or a spell's ingredients. Intuition is not one-size-fits-all. If everything is an expression of energy, then everything is in motion relative to everything else, and the ways those energies resonate—that is, are intuited—are unique to a practitioner.

When spellcrafting or practicing magick in general, it is crucial to only do the things that resonate with you, whatever really makes your intuition come alive. Pushing through anything that you do not fully believe in can become a chore, and the last thing anyone should want is for their magick to feel burdensome rather than a spirit-filled action meant to improve their lives.

If, for example, wearing pink is what absorbs and deflects negativity for you regardless of the common belief that black is the default color for this type of magick, then by all means wear all the pink you can and do what you have intuited is right for you as a witch. What works for you works for you.

Spellcrafting

What is a witch without spellcrafting? In a census taken by the online community Witch With Me in 2020, sixteen thousand witches answered a variety of questions. One of those questions was "do you cast spells?" A vast majority, nearly 84 percent of the witches who participated, said yes. In fact, only 10.7 percent responded with a flat-out no, while 5.3 percent were not sure.[17] The definition of what makes a witch a witch can vary from person to person, but statistics indicate that most witches cast spells. And it is safe to say a witch's intuition informs their spellcasting at some point in the process.

There are multiple avenues you can take when spellcasting. You can look up spells online or in a book and cast them exactly the way the spell is laid out. You might spend time researching different herbs to use for specific purposes or explore candle colors and moon phases in order to craft an original spell that is wholly yours. It is possible that you might talk with fellow practitioners to get their input while attempting to design the perfect spell. None of these processes is wrong. You can absolutely do one or all or none of these when preparing a spell. But there is something else that is consistently in play as you do any of this. Your intuition is leading you.

As you develop an understanding of your connection to your higher self you will find that your own particular witchy path becomes clearer. This is not to say that there are not many other byways that can be traveled; rather, the path your intuition leads you on is almost always the one that is most in line with your soul's purpose.

....

17 Meg Rosenbriar and Louisa Dean, "Witch With Me Census 2020," *Witch with Me* (blog), August 11, 2021, https://witchwithme.com/witch-with-me-census-2020-2/.

Spells can be about anything and look all sorts of ways. The only required component is you, the practitioner. Spell-crafting is an intricate process: to cast magick and manifest your desires, a spell must first make perfect sense to you as a witch. What does not ring true for you and your intuition is only going to distract you from your goals. Intuition plays such a vital role in magick because you have to be connected to what you are doing. Pay attention to your intuition; it will lead you to the right way of doing things for you regardless of what any books or other witches tell you.

Whether you follow a spell verbatim or completely wing it, listening to your inner guidance system allows you to make decisions based upon your insights about something. So, if a spell from the internet resonates with you exactly as it has been written, that is your indicator that this is the spell for you. And when things do not resonate with you it is a sure sign that you need to pay closer attention to what your intuition is telling you and then follow through on that message.

Use the Empowerment exercise "Silence Makes Your Magick Stronger" on page X as you develop your intuition in spellcrafting, using it as often as you need. It will help you not only develop confidence in your silence but also allow you to develop your intuition when creating spells that work for you.

Your Own Unverified Personal Gnosis

No conversation about intuition would be complete without a short discussion around the topic of Unverified Personal Gnosis, or UPG, the belief that a person's direct, transcendent experience of the Source is more authentic or truer than any belief or dogma that has been reached by community consensus. In other words, what you have discerned and know to be true for you supersedes any and/or all gnosis or spiritual knowledge that might exist in historical documents or grimoires or within any particular branch of the witchcraft community.

Say you have discerned that wearing pink absorbs and deflects negativity. That is an example of UPG. It is unverified; nowhere in any witchy history or literature are there any instances of pink absorbing or deflecting negativity. Instead it is personal knowledge you have discerned and know it works for you. What differentiates UPG from pure whimsy or caprice? UPG is a manifestation of your highly developed intuition. In the following chapter we will dive deeper into the differences between UPG and the wisdom we attain and look at how the two can work in concert with each other.

Intuition Leads to Wisdom

There are several different ways in which you can hone your intuition and intuitive skills, from growing your awareness of your clair senses to sharpening your divination practices. Developing your intuition into a supple and strong magickal tool does not cost you a dime. It does cost you time, focus, and energy.

Intuition is one way in which your energy is made manifest; in turn, it manifests your energy. When this energetic cycle is strongly flowing, it almost seems to sustain itself—as long as you keep paying attention. When your intuition is humming, wisdom becomes more readily accessible and attainable. It is with wisdom that you take the next step in developing a formidable magickal practice.

CHAPTER 3
Wisdom

Your intuition is informed by more than the divine connection you have with the world and universe around you. It is also shaped by knowledge gleaned from daily life. Your wisdom is interwoven with your intuition when you are spellcrafting, making your spells a dynamic fusion of the ineffable and the terrestrial. Wisdom comprises the insights you have fashioned from information you have received and continue to receive throughout your life. It is the distillation of what you have learned from a life lesson, the mechanism you use to make informed decisions, and the reservoir of knowledge you have obtained through surviving your hardships and celebrating your successes.

The wisdom you accumulate as you practice your spellcrafting is endless and vast. You might cast a spell that does not work; when you review the components, you are able to pinpoint the reason this magick failed you. It could be that you used components that did not jive well with your personal practice, or you ignored your intuition, or you might find that your goal was not well aligned with your path as a witch. The wise witch takes information as lessons learned from a spell's failure and incorporates that information into future spellcrafting, resulting in magick that works.

Understanding the world of witchcraft and its many traditional and nontraditional practices is vital to your development as a witch. It is only through gathering information that anyone is able to decipher which path they want to explore in depth. A firm knowledge base of folk magick, high magick, initiatory and lineaged paths equips a practitioner to make choices based on what their intuition has led them to understand is best for them. Additionally, a witch who is aware of a wide array of cultural practices is armed with wisdom on why those practices work. If so inclined, they can adapt or use different practices from a place of respect and understanding.

Using your wisdom and intuition in concert with each other is the most effective way to sustain a magickal practice that garners results. When you know how an herb or crystal works best for you, you are then able to adapt your wording, intention, and process to align your chosen components with the goal you plan to achieve through your spell.

The Difference Between Knowledge and Wisdom

"Knowledge is power." This aphorism is cliché for a reason: it's the truth. Everything you have ever learned, positive or negative, helps you not only grow but also adapt to the present and the future. As a mundane example, imagine you get a speeding ticket when driving down a street you have zipped through every day. Chances are that if you are learning, the next time you drive down that street you will pay close attention to your speedometer; if you don't, you will probably get another lesson in the form of another ticket. In other words, we may find ourselves repeating our mistakes until we learn the lessons buried within them. In short:

Knowledge: You have learned something and you now
know it

Wisdom: You apply what you have learned to other situations and experiences

The mundane lessons everyone learns in life will catapult a witch into a greater understanding of how the world around us functions. It is in learning that a bee stings or that flowers do not all bloom at the same time of year that we are able to shape our practice. You might think to yourself, "Well of course a bee stings and flowers don't all bloom at the same time; tell me something I don't know!" But stop. Wait. Think about it. Do not be too quick to dismiss what you might think is common knowledge. Successful spellcrafting takes what most people judge as common, mundane knowledge and looks a little more deeply into its properties. Having done so, a witch then seeks to recombine the elements of that knowledge in ways that honor and amplify the energies flowing all around us. In this way, advancing wisdom becomes foundational to a magickal practice. Like intuition, wisdom will inform everything that comes next in the lessons in chapters to follow. Understanding your world and your environment will help when you are foraging and finding. It will allow you to integrate what you intuitively understand into your intentions. And it is with wisdom that you eventually learn to fabricate the tools you deem necessary to your craft.

Developing Your Wisdom

Wisdom is one of those qualities that is not innate; you are not born with it. Instead, it is the result of cumulative and wide-ranging experiences. Everything that will ever happen to you will build upon all the other information that you have learned in life. For this reason, the most basic way in which we all develop our knowledge base from which we derive our wisdom is by going out and fully experiencing the world we live in to the best of our ability.

While there may always be information we do not have and may never know, we as a species are constantly attempting to know more and better understand all that the universe has to offer in terms of answers to our collective big-picture questions. It is in this search that we learn about moon phases, seasons around the world, astrology, and our own interaction with the energies around us. Through research and experimentation, we as a human family have learned about the world we live in and yet there are mysteries still undiscovered. When evolving our wisdom, the goal is to constantly reach for more information and ultimately seek out and assimilate that information into our daily lives. When we assimilate that knowledge into our compassion, discernment, and actions based on earlier experiences, we develop wisdom.

Life experience is one of the key ways most humans gain an understanding of our existence. Every scraped knee, broken bone, or traumatic experience we have has created a unique algorithm for each of us that further shapes our always evolving wisdom as we move forward in life. Everyone has some measure of wisdom. Even though there are aspects of information that are immutable and remain factual regardless of the viewer, there are characteristics of what we understand that are not so universally accepted. For example, some may know to the core of their being that a particular thing is true even when science has been proven that particular thing to be untrue over and over again.

Empowerment Exercise
From Mundane Knowledge to Magickal Wisdom

What you have learned throughout your life informs so much of how you view and move through the world. Often this knowledge is on such a subconscious level that you may not realize when, in an act of wisdom, you are applying what you've learned from one experience to other unrelated experiences. However, in the spirit of knowing thyself, we as practitioners would fall short of a truly magickal existence if we did not take the time to quantify how our mundane knowledge has informed our magickal wisdom.

Take time out of your day to examine your practice: How have you manipulated the practical knowledge you've gained—through school, work experiences, day-to-day relationships—and transformed it into magickal wisdom through the decisions you make and actions you take in your magick? What mundane information has helped to create your practice of witchcraft?

You do not need to write anything for this exercise; rather, simply ponder the questions. An answer might be that you have practical knowledge that the moon has phases. We as witches often pay attention to where the moon is in its transit. We know that the moon affects the tides and often our moods. Using intuition, many witches build their practice around these facts, and in doing so transform mundane knowledge into magickal wisdom.

Through identifying how your mundane knowledge intersects with your magickal wisdom you embrace the understanding that you are in dynamic relationship with the world and gain confidence in the skills you build as a completely unique practitioner. This self-exploration helps to peel away the veil that separates your magick life from your everyday one. It shows you how the knowledge you have gained through life experience has informed your wisdom as a witch. Ultimately this exercise will allow you to isolate the understandings you hold that in turn could demystify some of the roadblocks standing in your magickal path.

Discerning Your Truths

When sifting through all the information the world has to offer, you will soon realize that research must be part of your discernment process. Everything from the laws of physics to tying the perfect knot for a particular spell has been researched and examined to some degree. Your information warehouse can be built up more quickly when you dive into the scholarship of others who have come before you. Attending school or seeking out higher or further education are examples of building up a store of knowledge.

When seeking knowledge, it is important to verify the information you are receiving not only from an academic standpoint but from a personal one as well. For example, academically science tells us the earth is a sphere, but every one of us standing on this planet looks around and does not see the curvature of Earth's surface. Yet there are pictures taken from space that verify the fact that the Earth is a sphere. Fact-checking through multiple sources helps us accept that this is true even if we cannot see it ourselves.

From a personal standpoint, many times our discernment process can be influenced by the so-called spiritual or religious truths we have been taught. For example, in many faith traditions it has been passed down through countless years the statement that homosexuality is wrong. Faith teachings or dogma, particularly in the major world religions, are usually based on sacred texts that have gone through countless translations and interpretations across thousands of years. In the Christian Bible, for example, each translation through the millennia has subtly altered the meanings found in the original languages of the Bible: Hebrew, Aramaic, and Greek. When these languages are translated into, say, English, some of the passages end up being the best guess of the translator because not all of what was originally written matches the language it is being translated into word-for-word. Many times, these mismatches lead to real ambiguity in the teachings and text.

The Christian religion's view of homosexuality is an example of this textual ambiguity. Julie Mack, writer for the Kalamazoo Gazette, writes in "The 6 Bible verses on homosexuality, and differing interpretations" that among the verses:

> [The story of Sodom and Gomorrah] has been held up as a cautionary tale about the sinfulness of homosexuality. However, many scholars point to Ezekiel 16:49 as indicating that the cities were destroyed by God for not helping the poor and needy. Some also say the sinful sex occurring in Sodom and Gomorrah was rape, which means it doesn't apply to teachings on consensual same-sex relationships.[18]

18 Julie Mack, "The 6 Bible verses on homosexuality, and differing interpretations," *Kalamazoo Gazette* website, August 6, 2015, https://www.mlive.com/news /kalamazoo/2015/08/the_7_bible_verses_on_homosexu.html.

Are we then to assume that every sacred text of the world's major religions are all wrong and should therefore be repudiated? That is where your discernment comes in. Remember, wisdom does not evolve from only hearing information; it grows through learning to discern the personal truths that sometimes might be buried under a lot of noise.

At the end of the day, we can be faced with facts that are hard to swallow and information that does not feel accurate such that, after study and research, we can always refrain from incorporating whatever we wholeheartedly do not believe in. While there is always a line between what is absolutely true and what is absolutely false, sometimes this line is faded, hard to see, and/or thin. Other times this line is clear as day and easy to identify. When seeking wisdom, it is important to find these lines between fact and fiction for ourselves. We may sometimes end up on the wrong side of that line, and that is okay. As a human who is continually learning, you do not have to get it right the first time. Furthermore, your subjective opinions are likely to change as you expand and develop your knowledge base.

When it comes to developing wisdom, we should all always be active in our search and ready to shift as new information unfolds before us. We should be willing to accept that we were wrong if new knowledge shows us that our earlier understanding was incomplete. The quality of your wisdom is not always about how developed it is; more often, it is about how readily you can adapt to understandings that shift. Wisdom is not the body of everything you know—it grows from a constantly bubbling cauldron of facts and other data paired to your own understanding.

EMPOWERMENT EXERCISE
Adapting Your Wisdom

What is something that you once learned that you adapted and changed your understanding of over time? All of us are constantly changing. Even when you don't realize it, there are always processes that cause subtle changes to your personality, way of thinking, and even your magick. As an act of empowerment, consider the quality of your wisdom. Is it steadfast and immovable or is it more like liquid, flowing and ready to change course should new information come along?

When we first start learning about the world, our heads can be full of facts that we have yet to synthesize into wisdom. After we accumulate enough knowledge to function independently, we can begin to examine some of those facts more closely and play with new ways to fit all the pieces together; this is wisdom. We still gain knowledge, but as we mature we become more adept at and confident in creating unique insights from that knowledge. In this exercise, we ask you to think about how you have grown into your wisdom. Perhaps you used to think that the moon was following you when you were riding in a car but now you know that as the moon rises and the car speeds forward, the illusion that the moon is following you is simply that, an illusion. This is an example of a reinterpretation of facts after some wisdom has been gained.

What understandings of magick did you once hold that have evolved as you learned more about witchcraft? Identifying the ways in which your wisdom has developed and adapted to your new understandings of magick reminds you that adaptation is always possible. Fresh knowledge can expand and deepen your wisdom when you are open to the possibility that there will always be something new for you to learn.

Wisdom in Witchcraft

Witchcraft can have a lot of rules: use the moon in this way, open a circle, close a circle, this practice is closed, become initiated in this way. These rules have a valid place in our magickal community but here's the thing: you do not have to play by the rules. This is not to say that you should throw caution to the wind and do whatever you want whenever you want to do it with no forethought or basis for your decisions. On the contrary, you must understand *why* rules are in place. It is only after you fully grasp why rules exist and how they work that you can then break them creatively and effectively.

Wisdom gives us not only insight when spellcrafting but also a sense of respect for rules even when we choose to break them. Understanding why a waxing moon is good for calling things into your life helps to align your intentions with the specific energy the growing moon is naturally radiating. Knowing what a circle is and why it is cast provides background information when you are deciding what is vital to your practice.

Your witchcraft wisdom is developed from information you glean via a wide range of sources. Since the advent of the internet virtual classes and witchcraft schools have continued to expand in number and diversity. Social media is replete with specialized groups, hash tags, and multiple public figures verified with that little blue check. And of course, books continue to play a key role in developing the witching world's wisdom.

Sorting the Information

As mentioned earlier, wisdom comprises your understanding of the world and the knowledge you have gained. You are using your wisdom when you synthesize, combine, and recombine your knowledge in ways that enhance and strengthen your magick. The more knowledge you have—of the energies inherent in everything around you, how your own energies interact with the universe, and your life's purpose—the more robust your wisdom becomes and the more confident you will be when you decide to bend or break a few magickal rules.

Sorting through all the available information can seem like a daunting task. Training yourself to think in terms of the scientific method will help you sort what works from what does not. While we often think of this method as being confined to a laboratory setting, you can use the scientific method when analyzing all kinds of data from books to articles to podcasts and workshops.

Empowerment Exercise
Using the Scientific Method in Concert with Your Wisdom

The scientific method is a process based on observation and experience. It consists of the following steps:

Observe: Notice what happens

Question: Ask a question about what has been observed

Speculate: Form a hypothesis that you can test which might answer that question

> **Predict:** Make a prediction based on what you have
>   hypothesized
> **Test:** Test your prediction to see if it holds up
> **Expand:** Use your results to create new hypotheses

Observe

Witches are generally pretty plugged in to their environment, so chances are that you are already a somewhat keen observer of what is going on not only around you but also within you. Observations can be about anything that catches your special attention, whatever that makes you stop and wonder or go "huh."

For our purposes, let's say you observe that you seem to be highly energized by approaching thunderstorms. Instead of jumping or ducking like others seem to when thunder starts booming and lightning starts striking, you feel your pulse kick up not with fear but excitement with sizzling potentials and possibilities.

Write a short statement about your observation at the top of a sheet of paper or on your computer.

Question

Why is your experience of a thunderstorm so different from almost everyone else's? Under your observation statement, ask a question you have about what you have observed. It can be as broad or as narrow as you would like. Keep in mind that broad questions cast a wider net for answers.

Speculate

Here is where you begin to sort through possible answers to your question. Write as many possible answers as you would like; do not worry about making value judgements on what you write. The purpose here is to metaphorically dump out all of the possible answers from your mental answer bucket. You are speculating.

Read over your answers and choose the one that seems the truest, the most correct. Next, write down the spellcasting or magickal workings you think might be enhanced when done in concert with thunderstorm energies.

Predict

Continuing the example, you are trying to figure out why you are so energized by thunderstorms. The best hypothesis you have come up with is because you seem to be responsive to the changes in environment as a thunderstorm develops: the change in air pressure as evidenced by an uplift of wind, the sight of large, dark clouds, whatever you have observed. You have also jotted down some of the spells and/or magick you think might be enhanced using those energies.

Now it is time to make a magickal prediction based on what you have observed, the questions you have asked, and the spellwork or magick you think might be best to work during a thunderstorm.

Test

In this exercise, you will test your prediction the next time you know you will be in a thunderstorm by working whatever magick you hypothesized and writing down your observations after the magickal experiment.

Expand

Whether your magickal hypothesis stands up to testing or not, you have learned some new knowledge about how your magick works for you. When you incorporate what you have learned and build upon it, you are widening your sphere of wisdom.

When using this method as a tool for discernment, you can pare it down to fit almost any learning modality. Reading a book or taking a workshop? What do you notice happening to you as you read it or listen (observe)? Why are you having that response when the teacher or writer imparts a certain truth (question and speculate)? Can you think of other times you might experience the same response (predict)? If you read a book by a different author or take a workshop from an additional teacher, do you have the same response (test)? What conclusions can you make after sampling several different books or workshops, and how will the knowledge you have gained about that affect your future choices (expand)?

Remember: magick is all around us. By keeping notes on what knowledge resonates with you and how it does so, you are developing your confidence in your own sorting system of what is true most of the time, what is true some of the time, and what is never really true for you.

Magickal Traditions

In the book *How Witchcraft Saved My Life*, Vincent mentions that there is no wrong way to witch. This belief holds as true now as it always has and always will. The empirical evidence of this truth is borne out through the multiple magickal traditions that exist. We are all individuals and so of course there will be some traditions that resonate with us more than others. That makes sense, but if we only stick to those traditions that completely align with our beliefs and never explore the ideas and teachings of other paths that are available to learn from, we will not develop as fully as we might. Other traditions, whether integrated into our practice or not, are all valid. Taking the time to learn the magickal precepts of various systems and form a knowledge base of these paths can only enhance our understanding of how magick works in a multitude of ways.

High Magick and Folk Magick

High (or Ceremonial) magick is one expression of witchery from which wisdom may be gleaned. It is elaborate, intricate, and generally includes several elements and tools. It is fairly esoteric, rooted in Thelema, Hermetic Qabalah, and other philosophies. As with initiatory and lineaged practices, high magick follows a specific structure as taught to the practitioner by another practitioner.

Folk magick comprises a wide array of diverse magickal practices. This form of magick is typically practiced in more personalized ways as opposed to ceremonial magick. Initiation is not a requirement of folk magick, which is often passed down through familial or cultural lineage. Folk magick tends to be more practical in nature and is used to deal with everyday issues such as healing the sick, acquiring love, ridding oneself or others of evil, fertility issues, and other mundane life concerns.

Regarding folk or low magick, English historian Ronald Hutton writes that folk magick has been defined as being "concerned not with the mysteries of the universe and the empowerment of the magus [as ceremonial magic usually is], so much as with practical remedies for specific problems."[19] Despite the descriptors "low" or "folk," this magickal practice always has valuable wisdom to impart.

....

19 Ronald Hutton, *The Triumph of the Moon: A History of Modern Pagan Witchcraft* (New York: Oxford University Press, 1999), 84.

Wisdom Gained Through Initiatory and Lineaged Practices

In addition to books, classes, and workshops, knowledge and wisdom can be shared through participation in initiatory or lineaged covens. Gardnerian or Alexandrian covens, for example, teach particular ways of doing things and specific tools to use. We are only going to touch on this topic briefly only because there are a lot of lineaged practices in the witching community and they will be something you are going to encounter. If you are in a coven, it is almost a sure thing that much of what you will find in this book will not line up with what your High Priestess and High Priest have taught you, and that is absolutely to be expected—adhering to the practices of the craft as it has been handed down through coven leadership is crucial to maintaining the integrity of initiatory and lineaged covens. Yet even so, many of the teachings in this book will still be of use to you as you develop your individual practice.

One of the most amazing aspects of witchcraft is that it allows for the evolution of your practice. One witch may be born into a practice that has been handed down through generations that came before. A few years later, this same witch may find that none of what they were taught about magick resonates anymore. Another witch may have always worked only in coven magick or followed a highly structured set of laws but they have realized they would rather work alone and that their personal magick works best when they break the rules they were taught.

On the other hand, many witches begin their journey alone and are led from the heart and gut in all the magick they practice. Perhaps somewhere along the way, they realize that what they want is the structure of a coven and that having rules resonates with how they do magick. Ultimately, your magick is personal. There are a lot of crooked paths out there for you to explore in your search for what works best with your style of witchery. In general, one branch is not better than another; they are just different.

In older texts on witchcraft, it's commonly stated that a witch needs an athame, chalice, pentacle, cauldron, or wand, largely due to the fact that so many texts were centered around Wicca, founded by Gerald Gardner and Doreen Valiente in the 1940s and 1950s. To be clear, there are more than 1.5 million people who practice Wicca in the United States (a 2018 Newsweek article noted more people practice Wicca than there are members in the Presbyterian church).[20]

An initiatory or lineaged practice like Wicca imparts a lot of wisdom to the practitioner. Even if a coven is not the ultimate path for you, it is helpful to gain this wisdom. The more structured forms of witchcraft have impressive levels of practical and highly esoteric information. When you fully comprehend this wisdom, you are then able to move forward in making informed decisions about what your practice looks like. And if you do not know what Wicca is or the ways it is practiced, you cannot really say that these paths are not for you. It is only in understanding these various forms of practice that you can identify whether they resonate with you.

Upon learning about initiatory or lineaged paths, you will likely find that there are components of these traditions that have already made their way into your practice. And

....
20 Benjamin Fearnow, "Number of Witches Rises Dramatically Across U.S. As Millennials Reject Christianity," *Newsweek*, November 18, 2018, https://www.newsweek.com/witchcraft-wiccans-mysticism-astrology-witches-millennials-pagans-religion-1221019.

even if you choose not to strictly adhere to any of these ways of magick, you will likely find that some of what you have learned from Wicca will become integrated into your regular workings.

Jason Mankey, prolific Pagan writer and authority on witchy history, notes:

> What's been most surprising about many of those criticisms and dismissals of Wicca is that the people doing the mocking are essentially practicing Wicca. Celebrating the sabbats? The modern Wheel of the Year construct discussed above comes from Gerald Gardner, the world's first modern public Witch, and the person who first revealed to the world what we today call Wicca.... How's that ritual structure? Are you calling earth, air, fire, and water, casting a circle, and calling up a deity or two? Unless you are in the Golden Dawn, who were doing something similar first (though in a much more complicated manner), Wicca has had an impact on your practice.[21]

Again, Alexandrian, Gardnerian, or any number of initiatory magickal paths won't work for everyone, but you are going to find yourself hard-pressed to identify anything purely original (that is, not Wiccan) in your magickal workings. Whether you realize it or not, it is very probable that you are

....

21 Jason Mankey, "Wicca: Misconceptions & Misidentity" *Raise the Horns* (blog), February 2, 2021, https://www.patheos.com/blogs/panmankey/2021/02/wicca-misconceptions-misidentity/.

already participating in actions and practices that fall into both ceremonial and folk magick. Understanding why others are doing some of the same things you are is key to not only seeking community but also to applying these principles in more precise and focused ways.

Solitary Practice

A solitary practitioner is one who does not work within a group of witches. This means they do not work with a coven, nor are they likely to involve another witch in their practice. The boundaries for each solitary practitioner are as unique as the individual, so any rules about what they will and will not do with other witches vary greatly. A solitary practice can easily be lineaged or initiatory; it can be ceremonial magick or fall under a folk practice model. Solitary practices often do not fit into neat categories but instead tend to be tailored to the individual practicing magick. For this reason, it is not uncommon to find that a solitary witch is also an eclectic one.

Eclectic Practice

An eclectic practice is exactly what it sounds like—an eclectic witch typically draws from many different paths and creates their own tradition based upon a foundation of their own discernment. This tradition of magick is the most untraditional of the paths that have been covered so far. It is on this path that one often finds practices that are a mixture of both ceremonial and folk magick. As is the case with any magickal tradition, research is key, but it is particularly pertinent for the eclectic witch, as there is often no teacher or single guide to impart the ways of practice.

Because an eclectic path can and often does consist of the ideas found in many different practices, it can often span cultural divides. In this form of magick, it is just as possible for a practitioner to cast a circle when performing magick (Wicca) as readily as they might collect brick dust and place it in their door frames and windows (Hoodoo). An eclectic witch discerns and sets their own boundaries for their practice, making it unlikely that any two practices in this tradition will look identical.

The key to being a powerful eclectic practitioner is to always be sure that cultural practices are being appreciated and not appropriated. Because more than one culture is usually represented in this form of practice, it is vital for the practitioner to understand when and how to use any form of magick with origins outside of their own.

Cultural Appropriation versus Cultural Appreciation

A conversation about wisdom would not be complete without addressing cultural appropriation versus cultural appreciation, particularly as you fine-tune your practice to be an authentic expression of your personal magick. We bring this topic up because as you start deepening your practice, you will very likely experience times when you ask yourself whether what you are doing is cultural appreciation or appropriation.

Martha is about as white a woman as you will ever meet, with ancestors hailing from Ireland, Scotland, and England. She was raised in a city that has a very strong Mexican culture, including an annual week-long fiesta commemorating the Battle of the Alamo and the Battle of San Jacinto, in addition to annual events across the city celebrating Las Posadas, the pre-Christmas re-enactment of Mary and Joseph traveling to Bethlehem in search of lodging.

A couple of the Mexican traditions Martha grew up with included eating tamales on Christmas and New Year's Day, cracking *cascarones* (confetti-filled, decorated eggshells) on people's heads during the Easter season and making enormous tissue-paper flowers for Fiesta parades and celebrations. While Martha is not of Mexican heritage, she has a fairly good grounding in and appreciation of many Mexican customs and traditions. She does not present herself to others as Mexican, nor does she in any way profit from the culture monetarily. Those things would be appropriation.

The Difference Between Appropriation and Appreciation

Let's say you have decided to make a dreamcatcher like the ones in stores and online. You are pretty crafty, and they look fairly simple to make. You find some instructions, but there is a lot of blah-de-blah about the Ojibwe Nation—paragraphs of it!—before the actual instructions, and you do not want to spend any time reading that stuff! You just want to know how to make a dreamcatcher. So, you skip to the diagrams and get busy. Your finished product looks amazing! In fact, what you made looks so good that you think you might be able to make a few more and maybe sell them at the local farmer's market or on Etsy. Some time later, it turns out you were right; people love your dreamcatchers. While you certainly are not making enough money to quit your day job, you at least are not losing money and in fact are making a small profit. Plus, making them is a nice way to keep your hands busy while you watch television. Is this cultural appropriation or appreciation? What do you think?

Now let's say you have decided to make a dreamcatcher like the ones you have seen at stores and online. You are pretty crafty, and they look fairly simple to make. You start to do some research using reputable sources and learn that dreamcatchers are believed to have originated from the Ojibwe Nation (also known as the Chippewa, self-named the Anishinaabe) and that these creations are not universally Native American. During your research, you discover that dreamcatchers were used as protective talismans against bad dreams and nightmares, usually for young children. You learn about why they are designed the way they are and read a story on how bad dreams are "caught" in the dreamcatcher's web and destroyed by the rays of the morning sun.

You spend some time thinking about what you have learned and decide whether a dreamcatcher is a good fit with your spiritual practice before gathering your materials. Before you get started, you offer thanks for the knowledge you have gained and set whatever intention you have decided to imbue into your dreamcatcher. While you are crafting, you envision how your intention will manifest, perhaps chanting a small rhyme as you complete each component.

Your finished product looks amazing! You find the perfect place to hang it in your room, where you can see it first thing every morning. A few days later, a friend visits and notices it. They ask if you could make one for them, too. You decline but offer to teach how to make their own while sharing what you have learned about Ojibwe culture. Cultural appropriation or cultural appreciation? What do you think?

Maybe you are sick to death of hearing about cultural appropriation. We would venture to guess that if this is true, you are probably not from a culture that has been routinely appropriated: Afro-Cuban; various African, Asian, Hispanic, and Indigenous cultures, Romani; and so many more. What we are suggesting is that if you choose to incorporate a particular practice that is not native to your own culture into your magickal practice, please be mindful and do your homework before just grabbing at practices that look cool. Remember that just because you *can* take something does not mean you *should*. This is wisdom.

The discussion around cultural appropriation is a highly active one in the witchcraft community. There is a solid reason for this. Magick has lineage even if you are not in a lineaged practice. It is a gift that has been handed down through our ancestors. Cunning folk, nursemaids, shamans, medicine people, and many others figured out how to use the energies of the world around them to effect the changes they intended. They developed practices to heal and help those who needed it and to harm those who deserved it. We would be hard-pressed to find a single ancient culture in the world that was not influenced in some way by the beliefs and folklore handed down by their older wisdom-bearing generations. The apotropaic practices of Mediterranean culture are steeped in ideas specifically relevant to them, and the same is true for the many diverse cultures of Asia and their luck practices as it is for Afro-Caribbean descendants and their cosmologies.

When a practitioner begins to develop their aptitude, they are often drawn to specific practices, at least at first. Many incorporate aspects of the cultural systems they learned from their family members, some of whom do not necessarily practice witchcraft at all. As the witch comes into their practice, they sometimes begin to adapt the cultural aspects they have always known, specifically tailoring them to their practice. This is their culture shining through.

On the other side of the same coin, witches often begin to find their way to new and interesting ideas that may resonate with them for what are at first unknown reasons, for example Caucasian witches who are drawn to Hoodoo. Conjure, or Rootwork, is a practice created and practiced by enslaved Africans during a very bleak portion of our human history. At its core, Hoodoo was created to protect a disenfranchised and marginalized people. As University of Georgia graduate student Megan Lane writes: "Haitian slaves recognized early on that in order to preserve their culture in an oppressive and alien environment, they would need to adapt their beliefs to exist 'under the radar,' so to speak, of their Christian European captors."[22] The focus on protection magick is evident in several spells typically found in the practice: from averting the eyes of the law to warding the home against violence, the clear intention for safety is evident in this path.

There are many who strongly believe that only descendants of African people of color should participate in this form of magick. However, if we look at the typical practices of almost any modern American witch, it's common to find some form of Hoodoo represented at least in some amount. The United States is a salad bowl: a big mix of unique and distinct cultures. The line between what was handed down

....

22 Megan Lane and Sandy Dwayne Martin, *Hoodoo Heritage: A Brief History of American Folk Religion* (Atlanta: University of Georgia, 2008), 26.

through family and what energies have been active in the environment where a witch lives is often, at best, blurred.

The question persists: if we, you, or anyone else were to start using brick dust in our doorways and windows as a form of protection, are we appropriating a culture (assuming we are not a member of that culture)? The simplest answer is: not necessarily. If your intentions are sound, you are respectful, and you have found information that resonates with you, then the practice is meant for you. This is of course *only* after you fully understand the reasons why this particular action works in the magickal application you intend it for.

There is so much in the universe that we do not understand or cannot definitively answer with absolute certainty. Whether we live multiple lives or ascend to "heaven" when we die will likely always be a mystery. Even so, there are hypotheses proposing that one might be drawn to a particular form of spellcraft or work because they have had a previous life or lives in the culture from which the practice is derived. If a person is doing their best in this life to appreciate the culture from which the practice came, it is no one else's business or place to judge whether or not participation in a particular way of witching is acceptable.

Empowerment Exercise
Are You Appreciating or Appropriating?

In this exercise, we ask you to look deeply into your practice to identify how much you really know about the aspects of other cultures that have worked their way into your witchcraft. Are you being appreciative of a cultural practice or are you appropriating it?

To begin, identify which practices you employ that are not original to your own culture. You can list these on paper, on your phone, or on a computer. You may find it helpful to list your spell components and each step of casting the spell as part of this process.

Next, examine where you learned the practices you are using. Did you read about them somewhere? Were they learned through a conversation? Or are they something that just came to you, and you have no idea where you learned to do the things you are doing? There are no wrong answers here; you are simply fact-gathering.

Once your list is complete, begin doing some research on the types of magick you employ. If you find some information about that practice, explore it. For example, is there another culture that uses eggshells in the same way you do? Do eggshells have magickal uses in more than one culture? If the answer is yes, examine the similarities and differences between the practices, including your own. If your use of eggshells lines up with the practice of a culture that is not your own, take a careful look at the reasons you are employing that particular spell. Is it because of how it looks or how it works? If it's the latter, you have an ethical responsibility to learn all that you can in order to understand this practice within its cultural context. If you find you have picked up the practice mostly because it adds to your cool witchy vibe you may want to consider finding a new way to work your spell that does not infringe on a particular way a specific culture manifests their magick.

This exercise is a key component in developing both your magickal signature and a witchcraft practice that is free of appropriation and full of appreciation for cultures that are different from your own.

When Wisdom Tells You to Break All the Rules

Once you have done your research and learned more than the bare minimum on any subject matter, you can then employ your wisdom to mix things up a little bit. Knowing the phases of the moon is great, using those phases in alignment with the energy that they present at the given time is helpful. But what do you do when you have a spell to cast that does not line up with the phase of the moon you are in?

It is not necessary to work with the moon in your spellcraft. It can help but you are not going to lose your witching license if you do not use the moon in its present phase. That said, for the witches who prefer to use the moon there is a way to work around a phase that does not match your intention. Just because the waxing moon is good for calling in your desires does not mean you have to wait for a waxing moon to cast a spell to manifest something. You simply manipulate the phrasing of your intention and adapt it to fit the energy of the moon. The next chapter explores into this idea in more detail. For now, keep in mind that there is a flipside to every spell. Instead of calling something in, you may find that you must release something that aligns precisely with what you desire. For instance, if you are calling in a new job but the moon is not in the correct phase, you could consider releasing your current job. You could also release the fear of not getting hired at the new job or anything else that lines up with letting go on a waning moon while also aligning with getting that new position.

Magickal rules were meant to be broken. Once you understand why they are in place, once you have a firm grasp of what the rules protect you from or regulate, you can then make the choice to go against the grain and do your magick your way.

Empowerment Exercise
Find a Rule to Break

Most of us do not always want to follow all the rules all the time. Take a moment to identify a magickal rule that you have been following in your spell casting. This could be something simple like stirring your coffee clockwise in the morning as you imbue an intention into it or as complex as creating and burying a witch jar for protection.

Examine the rules about the practice and research the reasoning behind them. This might send you down a rabbit hole of information. Follow the rabbit hole and see what wonders are on the other side. It will be worth it in the end.

After completing your research on that magickal rule, consider how you can effectively break or bend it to your will and why you might choose to do so. For example, maybe you will start to work with what you already have or what is readily available instead of making a special purchase. However you decide to bend or break the rule, notice how the manifestation feels when you cast the spell in this new way. Take note of how you feel after breaking that rule and examine the results of the spell you have cast. If personalizing your magick resonates with you, develop new ways to continue learning why the rules exist and then begin to bend or break them to align with your magickal DNA.

Magick is born out of necessity. It does not always fit into a tidy box with the "right" materials or the perfect astrological positioning for your workings. Learn how to identify a rule first then find a way to work around it. This is one of the most empowering things you can do to move your spellcasting forward.

A Witch May Wander

There is an old saying that wisdom listens, and it is a key component of developing your wisdom. Listen. Ask questions to learn more. Seek new experiences and hone your awareness of the world around you. Employ the scientific method as you gather the wisdom you need to empower your practice and keep a record of what you have learned as you seek answers to your questions.

Go out to find information on all the paths a witch may wander, even from sources and traditions you are pretty sure you will not be following exactly as presented. As you develop your knowledge base, begin to construct your own path. An informed practitioner is a powerful practitioner. Use the power you gain through developing your wisdom to better both your practice and you. Melding multiple journeys into one uniquely personal path empowers you to be the dynamic spark that fully activates and increases your own magickal aptitude.

CHAPTER 4

Intention

It is currently a popular belief that a witch only needs their intention to manifest their desired goals. While there is some truth to this, a generally agreed-upon process exists for a reason. Is it truly spellcrafting if a witch simply speaks their intention without any additional energy directed toward the manifestation of that intention? If a witch learns about a job and says, "I am going to get that job" and leaves it at that, is that witchcraft? After all, isn't that an example of speaking their desire aloud? Isn't articulating your intention what witchcraft is all about?

Intention completes the trifecta created when partnered with intuition and wisdom. Certainly, you can set an intention without employing wisdom and/or intuition and still see that intention manifested. But when your intentions are reinforced with wisdom and a deep knowing that they will come to fruition, your power skyrockets into the universe and your desires become that much more achievable.

The dualistic nature of your intention is one of the most powerful aspects of how you communicate in both the mundane and magickal realms. The ways you choose to actively interact with your surroundings, including what you speak into existence, work together to shape your reality. In essence, the power to be a co-creator of your reality lies within you.

Perception Is Reality

Psychologist and Life Coach Dr. Linda Humphreys has said, "Perception molds, shapes and influences our experience of our personal reality. Perception is merely a lens or mind-set from which we view people, events, and things."[23] So the question becomes, what influences your perception?

The way we perceive things around us both remotely and directly is shaped in part by our past experiences and to some extent by our predispositions and beliefs about what is true. Although every person has a unique perception of reality, we tend to think of a person whose perception has wandered too far away from reality as delusional. Yet reality and perception are not necessarily always in direct conflict with each other, and it is our perception that helps us understand reality. Honing your powers of perception strengthens your ability to peel back the layers that might be obscuring the reality around you. The sharpness of your perception directly impacts the ways you choose to create and shape your intention.

From Intangible to Tangible

Of the three intangibles we have discussed—intuition, wisdom, and intention—intention has a unique quality. Intuition and wisdom are both purely intangible; that is, there is not really any particular thing or object we can point to or hold in our hand that is the unadulterated, 100-percent embodiment of intuition or wisdom. A case could be made that certain books can be considered an embodiment of a particular wisdom, but a witch's wisdom does not reside solely in books and does not

....
23 Jessica Estrada, "How Your Perception is Your Reality, According to Psychologists" Well + Good website, February 7, 2020, https://www.wellandgood.com /perception-is-reality/.

seat itself within an isolated branch of wisdom. Witches tend to be free-range wisdom-gatherers. Intention further differentiates itself from intuition and wisdom not only in its function but also in how it functions.

Intention is a powerful bridge between magickal and mundane realms. It is the connector between your inner magickal garden—the realm where the seeds of your intention are nurtured and cultivated—and the outer reality you physically inhabit. As such, intention has both intangible and tangible aspects. One of the processes by which it can be made manifest is through aligning your intentions with your magickal energies and vice versa.

To be clear, we mean "intention" as both a noun and a verb. The intention that you decide you will manifest is an intangible thing; when you take steps to manipulate that intangible thing so that it becomes activated in the world, that intention becomes tangible and is infused with energy. Intention is not unlike the final two stages of a butterfly's life. When you conceive an intention, it is in a pupal state within the chrysalis of your mind; as that intention is developed and brought forth into the world, it enters its complete, or butterfly, state and flies out into the world.

Capturing Intention

Very often, a witch knows the outcomes they seek to achieve, but the intention part of the equation can sometimes be as slippery as an eel to pin down and hold in place, even for the most seasoned of practitioners. This is not a failure by any means; it is an opportunity. When you capture your intention, defining as precisely as you are able what it is you intend to achieve, you are then able to interlace that intention into the vision your higher self is conjuring to life. This careful attention to detail produces magick that garners results. Success lies in first identifying your intention and then being as specific as possible with exactly what you are attempting to manifest.

Honing an Intention

Honing your intention is vital for the success of any spell you may cast. This means that the intention you release into the world must be carefully constructed and surgically precise. For example, it is one thing to say that you want money. The intention may sound clear, but why do you want the money, how do you want to receive the money, and what amount of money do you require? Do you want a single lump sum or are you looking to obtain a sustainable income that will stabilize your life? Is there any sort of timetable in play? Do you want the money to come from a specific source, such as payment owed to you or income from being a professional witch? The answers to these types of questions will help you to hone an intention that accurately aligns with the energies you are preparing to launch into being. As you sharpen the focus of your intention, it may come to light that it is not money you want so much as you are seeking to put into place a specific set of conditions that result in a measurable increase of money in your hands.

Specificity Is Powerful

The most powerful spells that you can cast are often the ones that are the most specific. This is because the intention becomes so razor sharp that there is little to no margin of error. In other words, the more scrupulous you are in setting your intentions, the more likely you are to see them come into fruition. Being specific is integral to successful spellcasting because it empowers you to be laser-focused on exactly what you want.

Empowerment Exercise
Honing and Specifying Your Intentions

With a pen and a piece of paper, express your intention in words. Based on the example in this section you would write, "I need money" first. Then take a moment to answer questions about that money. Some examples of questions you might ask yourself: What is the money for? Is there a specific sum that is needed? Do I need it by a certain date? Do I only need to obtain this money one time? Is it for a particular expense that will not arise again? Am I making enough money to live the life I desire? How can I make this money?

As you write the answers to questions that are relevant to your intention, clarity will begin to develop. You may discern that what you actually need is a different or additional job. Or you could realize that you only require a short-term loan from a parent or friend. You may come to realize that it is not that you need money to support your everyday expenses—what would instead best serve your needs is a windfall, a short-term part-time gig, or whatever else it is that your answers lead you to.

Do not be surprised if the refined intention does not seem to match the first draft of your intention. What you will find is that the final iteration of your honed intention still addresses the desire expressed in the initial draft but in a way that aims your will toward your goal with precision and power.

Words Are Magick

Since you are reading this (or any) book we can assume that you probably respect the power inherent in words. It should not come as a surprise that the power of words is a crucial component of highly effective magick. No matter how we pronounce them, words convey meaning. Even more amazing is that the meaning carried in a single word can be subtly yet profoundly altered depending on one's location, dialect, inflection, intention, and countless other factors.

As an example, think of a simple word like "hello." Now think of all the different ways you can say that word and change its meaning even though the word itself does not change one iota. Hello! (enthusiastic) Hello? (questioning) HELL-o! (surprised) Hello. (impersonal) This one word can be said seductively, brusquely, sarcastically, hopefully—any number of ways, each of which impacts the meaning, or the intent, of the word.

Think of the emotion a poet expresses in their art. The language of poetry is the language of metaphor; a well-crafted poem leaves enough room for the reader to actively engage in meaning-making because the reader is invited to bring something of themselves to their interpretation of the poet's words. The poet's words and phrasing are precisely selected with the intent that those words and phrases have enough porosity in their meaning such that readers can draw their own insights. For this reason, successful poetry never reads the same way twice; it is a living thought-form that subtly changes in accordance with what the reader brings to it with each reading. If the words of a poet can actively engage a reader and can elicit fresh insights, what might the words of a witch do?

Whether you have mispronounced a word, spelled it wrong, or have perfect diction is less important than the energy you are putting into the idea the words embody. This all leads to a specific practice many witches are familiar with: writing intentions.

Magick In Pen On Paper

Think of intention-writing as part of your witchy *mise en place*, a French culinary term meaning "putting in place" that refers to the setup of both food and kitchen equipment prior to cooking so that the actual cooking time isn't interrupted. When you write your intentions, you are essentially putting every aspect of them in place and ready to go. That way, when you get to the part of the ritual in which you activate the intention's manifestation, you can do so with all of your attention and focus directed toward that manifestation.

The Hebrew phrase *ebrah k'dabri* means "I will create as I speak."[24] Some believe this is where the word "abracadabra" originated. The Aramaic term ארבדכ ארבא can be translated to "I create like the word."[25] In both instances, the belief that words contain the power of creation is evident.

The written word conveys a sense of solidification. Words bring our metaphysical thoughts into the physical world. We focus our minds to create rules and standards that, when written, we often believe it must be so. Many people believe something must be true if they read it, no matter how far-fetched it might be. Words create realities that are sometimes wildly fantastical and other times based in verifiable actualities. They

....

24 Michael Quinion, "Abracadbra," Worldwide Words website, updated December 19, 2005, https://www.worldwidewords.org/qa/qa-abr1.htm.

25 Seth Balthazar, "Abracadabra: 'As I Speak, I Create,'" Seth Balthazar's website, April 18, 2021, https://sethbalthazar.com/2021/04/18/abracadabra-as-i-speak-i-create/.

give us insight into the world around us and often shape our truths (our perceptions) whether we realize it or not.

Harnessing the power of words made manifest is an ability any witch can develop. You need only to believe to your utter core in what you have written and then send that intention or spell out into the world with every fiber of your will. You must hyper-focus your will to give birth to your beliefs and then incubate them into reality.

Inscribing words on anything can easily become a spell in its own right. For instance, it is a common practice in sweetening spells to write the name of one's target and then one's own name on a slip of paper while imbuing the inscription with an intention before submerging the names into the sweetener. There are countless spells wherein the caster first writes on a piece of paper the things they want to either banish or call in and then burns the list, transmuting their desires into smoke that dissipates into the ether.

Once an intention is crafted, inscribing it into a candle or on paper or a leaf becomes the first physical act of drawing that intention into existence. Essentially the practitioner is saying, "This is real. I can see it and I have made a concrete connection between my desire and the act of magick I am performing." Words can be thought of as vehicles that convey power in a tangible way. They are little dump trucks filled with your energy or intention.

Writing out an intention is a simple act of magick. You have lots of options when performing this kind of spell. In witchcraft, everything from writing in a journal to writing down and sending your wishes off in the smoke can be a ritual of manifestation. Writing your intention is fundamental to the casting of your spell; in fact, it is so foundational that often mindfully scribing your intention onto paper can be the only step needed.

Let's say you are writing a list of negative qualities you want to banish from your life. You start by bringing those qualities to the forefront of your mind, organizing or drawing them together, which can be thought of as a type of visualization. As you write each quality down, you are creating a directional energetic flow from you through the writing implement to the paper where those qualities are captured or held in stasis. With each negative quality you write, that little dump truck energetically returns to you, ready for another load of negative qualities (or whatever your intention happens to be). What you are doing is dumping those negative qualities you want to banish from your life onto the paper, the first step in ridding yourself of them energetically. Think of how you feel when you reach the end of the list, when you have emptied yourself of all the negative qualities you could think of. Through the action of writing the words, you have started to exercise some control over those qualities. And, having some control over them, you can do with them as you will—this is the essence of magick.

Writing Down Your Magick

After identifying and honing your true intention (see the Honing and Specifying Your Intention Empowerment exercise on page 113), transcribe the final draft of that statement onto a fresh piece of paper. This action is another step in drawing your will out from your inner garden of ideas and potentials into the physical world where it will become manifest. Think of your inner garden as anchoring one end of a metaphysical tether; when you write down the words of your precisely honed intention you are essentially pinning the other end of the tether down into the physical world, creating an energetic strand that connects the concept inside you to what is around you, a strand upon which your intention physically moves toward manifestation. With the power that words hold, writing your magick out so that you can see it, touch it, smell it, and taste it is an ideal way to empower the manifestation of your desires. There are myriad ways to put this practice into action. From creating a simple list placed on an altar to carving words into a candle or even creating sigils with words or symbols, you can harness the power of words.

Simple phrases or even a single word can direct your intention into its most manifest reality. Once you have a clearly identified path you want to follow, these words can be used as a metaphorical guiding light. Since magick through intention setting is so supple, even creating a sort of shopping list of all the goals you are applying your magickal energies toward is a powerful and effective way to keep you on task.

Empowerment Exercise
Write It Down to See Daily

Once you have honed your specific intention, you can simply write it out and place it where you will see it every day, on a dry-erase board, a piece of paper, or even with lipstick on a mirror. The exercise is not about what you are writing the intention on as much as it is about the act of seeing your intention regularly.

When you place the intention in an easily visible spot, you are not only setting the intention but also giving yourself a reminder that this intention is becoming manifest. That daily reminder scrolled out in luscious apple on your mirror or penned neatly and taped to your desk at work will serve as a visual representation that you are nurturing something to fruition. When you can see the written words of your magickal goals they remind you that your intention will become concrete.

Words on Bay Leaves

Bay leaves are magick almost solely on their own. Also known as laurel, bay leaves appear in both ancient Greek mythology and ancient Roman practice. Parthenius of Nicaea wrote:

> [The Naiad-nymph Daphne,] seeing Apollon advancing upon her, took vigorously to flight; then, as he pursued her, she implored Zeus that she might be translated away from mortal sight, and she is supposed to have become the bay tree which is called daphne after her.[26]

Laurel crowns were worn as a symbol of triumph. The Romans, liking this Greek practice, adopted it as their own.[27]

And in *Medicinal Plants of South Asia*, published online by the US National Library of Medicine, we find:

. . . .

26 Parthenius, Daphnis and Chloe by Longus; *The Love Romances of Parthenius and Other Fragments*, trans., J. M. Edmonds and S. Gaselee (Cambridge, MA: Harvard University Press, 1935), 1.

27 "History at Home: Laurel Wreath Activity" *History Museum of Mobile* website, n.d., https://static1.squarespace.com/static/59fc7cafbff200c34f972a81/t/5e95dbb710c89d708989fd72/1586879418672/LaurelWreathActivity.pdf.

> The Temple of Delphi, dedicated to Apollo, used many bay leaves. The roof was made of bay leaves, and priestesses would have to eat bay before giving their oracles. This may have been aided by bay's slightly narcotic qualities. Thus, bay leaves are said to aid with psychic powers, particularly prophetic dreams, clairvoyance, protection, healing, purification, strength, wishes, magic, exorcism, divination, visions, inspiration, wisdom, meditation, defense, and accessing the creative world.[28]

In fact, evidence of that ancient respect for the magickal power of bay laurel pops up in our conversations to this day: the honors of Poet Laureate, Baccalaureate, and the concept of "resting on one's laurels" are just a few examples. A pantry staple for most cooks, bay leaves are easily obtainable at your local grocery store.

Wise women and cunning men have been aware of the power of the bay laurel since ancient days. When reading spells authored by different witches across the years, you will find that a bay leaf can be used for almost anything magickal from protection to manifestation and well beyond. It may come as no surprise that these dynamic leaves can be carriers of potent magick with just a word or two written on them. Having a rather spicy, peppery flavor, bay leaves correspond to sun energies.

....

28 Muhammad Asif Hanif, Haq Nawaz, Muhammad Mumtaz Khan, Hugh J. Byrne, eds. "Bay Leaf," in *Medicinal Plants of South Asia: Novel Sources for Drug Discovery*, (Amsterdam, the Netherlands: Elseveir, 2020), https://doi.org/10.1016/C2017-0-02046-3, 63–74.

Writing words on to bay leaves is a powerful spellcasting technique that helps to draw your intentions into the physical world. It allows the practitioner to not only see their intentions written out but to also align them with a potent magickal ingredient that has proven essential to magick-making for centuries. A simple word or phrase on the leaves can be inscribed with a marker and then burnt or carried with you in order to draw your intention into being.

EMPOWERMENT EXERCISE
An Intention for Clarity

To help you find clarity when defining your intentions, take a bay leaf and a use a fine-tipped marker to write the words "Clear Intentions." Once you have inscribed your bay leaf, you can proceed one of two ways: keep it in a safe place or burn it.

If keeping the inscribed bay leaf is most closely aligned with the way you choose to practice magick, you will want to make sure it is secured in a place where it will not be moved around or disturbed, as dried bay leaves are fragile. If it is disturbed, you can always inscribe another bay leaf. One magickally elegant way to ensure the safety and longevity of your inscribed bay leaf is to adhere it to a page in your book of spells or even tape it on top of your altar, which allows you to see the bay leaf and its inscription every time you begin to set your intentions while also ensuring it stays intact over time.

Take time to look at this bay leaf and remember that you are drawing in clarity as you craft the intention you are currently working on. You might write yourself a little charm to recite each time you look at the leaf, simply repeat the words inscribed on it, or perhaps even visualize the clarity flowing into you.

If you choose to burn your bay leaf, use metal tongs to hold the stem and make sure a fire-safe dish is set under it. Be aware that bay leaves can spark a little, so take care that you are in an open environment without other flammable items nearby. As you burn your bay leaf, focus on drawing clear intentions to yourself. You can use visualization if it comes easily to you, or you can simply chant the words if that works best. You may find that it is a best practice to burn your leaf prior to defining your intentions for each spell.

Burning Intentions into the World

For a moment, consider the power of fire: heat transforms a once-solid material into ash; literally nothing discernible is left behind. Some would describe this transformation as alchemical. There is power in the flame and its wild and untamed dance, yet it can be contained. Its very existence is dynamic—a gift from the gods indeed.

Picture a full moon: on a night like this, there is no need for a flashlight as all the world is bathed in the glory of reflected light from our celestial satellite. A witch searches the ground for twigs and dried leaves. Their goal is clear: they gather what is necessary to build a small fire. A pit, hand-hewn into the ground, holds the witch's findings. The fire is ignited and watched as it begins to grow. The costs of this ritual are only time and the annual sacrifice provided by autumn. Here are the makings of magick.

There are countless things our witch could plan to do in this scene. They could gaze into their fire to divine what should be released as the moon begins to wane in the next few days. The intention could be to send an offering up to a deity in the form of smoke. Or maybe this witch wants to bathe in the fire, using its energy and heat to cleanse and burn away what does not serve them.

But tonight, this witch carries with them a curled-up piece of paper, an intention written out and charged with their energy. The witch says a few words and places their scroll into the flame. As the paper burns, they see the smoke rising. They know with every fiber of their being that under the power of the full moon, their intention is released into the world and ready to manifest.

Fire is used to cook our food and warm our bodies. It is used to protect and sometimes destroy. Why would we not also use it to send our intentions into the ether? In spellcraft, fire becomes a gateway.

There is a liminal quality to fire that is very compelling to witches seeking to manifest their intentions. The energy of fire consumes and transforms; we can literally see our intentions being altered from one form to another. We can see the browning of the paper, then the blackening, the glowing red edges consuming the paper, the paper twisting and curling in response to the flames as if it were a living creature that rises—transformed—as smoke. As aware as we may be about the mechanics and the science of fire, there is still something mystical about those threshold moments between unburnt and burned to ash, between ash and its transmutation into smoke.

Writing out our magickal goals can be powerful, and combining that power with the alchemy of sending them off in fire our intentions become transformative. Whether written on a bay leaf or a piece of parchment, setting an intention aflame helps to remove it from the mortal plane. Fire allows that intention to enter the world of spirits and deities; the spell becomes ethereal, and it is on this plane that our work gains traction. Burning our written intentions is the final step in sending our magick out. It gives the witch an opportunity to see the spell begin to take shape.

With any form of spellcasting, it is always critical to let go once the process of manipulating our manifestations into the world. This does not mean we stop thinking about them or that we do not have to continue to work for our goals. Rather, we center ourselves in a confidence that our intention is set and now in the hands of the Source we work with. When we burn our words the catharsis we feel indicates that we have done exactly that: placed our expectations at the altar of the power we draw from and released ourselves of the need to worry whether we will see our magick develop into real-world outcomes.

We free ourselves when we burn our spells, as though we are saying, "Okay, that's it. The spell is complete." The burden of wanting can be relieved when we send our magick out in the transformative heat of a fire. We understand that this desire we have, these things or goals we want to gain or achieve, are not only ours anymore. We have shared them, sent them away as if planting a seed that we know will be harvested when the time has come.

EMPOWERMENT EXERCISE
Sending Your Intentions Out in Fire

Discern and define an intention using any of the methods covered in this chapter or in a way of your own devising. Write the final distillation of your intention on a piece of paper or a bay leaf. Once your intention is captured and pinned down, find a place where you can safely work with fire. You may need a fire-safe dish, a fire pit, or a space cleared of anything that might ignite. Always remember that working with fire can be dangerous and should only be done with extreme caution.

In your fire-safe space, bring the flame to your written intention either by simply throwing the intention into a fire or by lighting a corner of paper with a match or lighter. As your intention burns, know that it is moving from the physical realm into the ethereal. You can visualize this transformation or simply speak a statement of the intention's transformation out loud. You may want to mention which deity, if any, to whom you are sending this intention.

As the fire burns, you can either imagine or talk about how this intention should play out. Is the intention for you to win the lottery? What numbers will you play? What are the details of the scene when you find out you are a winner? Or maybe your intention is to get a book deal. What will the email say when you are told the publishers are moving forward with your idea? Take the time to mentally paint a picture of exactly how this intention will look and feel when it has manifested.

Another Aspect of Intention

Remember: intention has a dual nature. It is not just the things we want or seek in the world—it is also the energy we place into the items and tools we use in our practice.

It is profoundly empowering to realize that the plastic top of a milk jug can in fact hold the energy a practitioner chooses to place there just as well as any crystal brought home from the local witch shop. This is not to say that the crystal does not have powerful potential but rather, if not charged, that crystal holds no greater power than the mundane little red top sealing your milk in its container.

Does a crystal have a higher vibration than a little plastic cap? Probably, but without your conscious choice to place your intention into it and without you directing your power into it, that crystal is just another rock. Remember, we witches can use whatever items we need to help focus our power, and the creative use of our intention is the way we do that.

Focus Objects

In many witchcraft traditions, the athame is typically associated with fire. Vincent is a fire witch, and the element had called to him since before he even began to practice. At first, he thought he had to have a blade of some sort to magickally connect to this element that is so intrinsic to who he is. But he never acquired an athame yet is still very much a witch who works with fire as an elemental enhancer in his magick.

All sorts of things correspond with the elements in magick. Plants, planets, zodiac signs, and of course, tools. A focus object does exactly what it sounds like: it allows you to enhance your power by channeling it through an object. Using this concentrated force, you send out your power wrapped around an intention like a seed safe and nourished in the soil. As your spells receive metaphysical nutrition from this focused energy they blossom and manifest into fruition, ready to harvest. It is not the star anise on your altar that enhances your sacred space; rather, it is your desires, your energies that coalesce with focus objects to manifest pure, concentrated, and focused intentions. The star anise itself has some inherent magickal energy, but without your magickal intention harnessing and amplifying its energies, the star anise is simply an ingredient for pie or fancy café drinks.

The plant known as witch hazel (*Hamamelis virginiana*) is another example of a focus object. Native Americans along the eastern coast of what is now known as the United States used it as an eye medicine, a kidney aid, and a cold remedy. Early American settlers used witch hazel as a medicinal tea, and the branches of the tree were commonly used for divining where water or minerals such as ore or metals might be located (this is known as dousing, or water-witching, hence the non-indigenous name given to the tree). It is believed that the Mohegan tribe of Connecticut first demonstrated to English settlers how to use Y-shaped witch hazel sticks for dowsing.[29] Modern-day dowsers might use metal rods, copper wire, or other materials, but back in the day the go-to material was wood cut from the peach tree, the willow tree, and witch hazel.

Note that the forked tree branch does not just wiggle under its own power over to the site where the water is (although that would be something to see!). The person wielding the

....

29 Aimee Regur, "Witch Hazel—Hamamelis virginiana" PangeaOrganics website, February 28, 2017, https://pangeaorganics.com/blogs/pangea-blog/witch -hazel-hamamelis-virginiana?_pos=1&_sid=3b6ca7abc&_ss=r.

forked tree branch uses its energies to focus and enhance their own energies as they search for water. We view magickal tools the same way. One of the witch's tasks is to learn about the magick in the world around them and then to select their tools in accordance with their own intentions using materials that will best enhance those intentions.

Let's look at one more example: quartz crystals. In "How to Use Crystals to Generate Electricity," Eli Laurens writes:

> Crystals, such as quartz, can be tapped for electricity using a piezoelectric (mechanical energy discharge) method. By securing the crystal and subjecting it to direct force with a permanent magnet, a detectable amount of electricity is released. This technology is used in cigarette lighters and gas grill ignition buttons; the unit requires no battery cell to operate. Continuously rapping on the crystal will produce usable electrical current.[30]

Where the average person sees a pretty rock, both the scientist and the witch see a source of energy. Both of us use crystals to help focus our magickal workings, yet crystals and wands and sigils and incense and athames and pentacles and all of the bits and bobs of magick-working notwithstanding, at the end of the day, we witches already have every tool we need within us. The earth, the air, the fire, the water, the Spirit—all of it. "Witchcraft" is simply the term we use when

....

30 Eli Laurens, "How to Use Crystals to Generate Energy" Sciencing website, March
    13, 2018, https://sciencing.com/use-crystals-generate-electricity-6729045.html.

we are working with and activating all these elements with will and intention supported by wisdom and intuition.

Intention in Tools and Objects

Whether you have purchased the most expensive ritual tool or crafted something yourself, items do not hold any power in addition to their intrinsic energy signatures until you open the metaphysical door and complete the magickal connection.

Our magickal tools hold power for two reasons. First, because we believe that they do, these items gain an additional element to their energy signature that both enhances and is enhanced by our personal connection to them. Since the magick is in you and you are the magick, your tools can be made powerful by the magick you place in them.

Second, magickal tools are often something that we have spent time learning about. Whether a crystal or a knife, we have discerned through education whether an item aligns with our magickal practice. While we may have first been drawn to a tool by our curiosity and knowledge-gathering, somewhere along the way our wisdom and our intuition worked together to cement that tool as our preference for use in spellcasting.

Witchcraft is malleable. It can be shaped to fit both your needs and your access to ingredients. If what you have available is vegetable oil when you are dressing a candle in a spell that calls for extra virgin olive oil, you can still use the vegetable oil without any loss of magickal potency. If the spell you are crafting is about luck and clovers from your yard resonate with you as lucky, you can go right outside and pluck a clover from the ground to use in your spell.

In the 2017 Marvel Studios movie *Thor: Ragnarok*, Odin has an exchange with Thor during the latter character's bleakest moment, when he and all of Asgard are facing sure defeat at the hands of his deadly cinematic sister, Hela. Thor, having lost his mighty hammer Mjölnir, is literally brought to his hands and knees by his overwhelming sense of powerlessness. Odin responds, "Are you Thor, the God of Hammers? That hammer was to help you control your power, to focus it. It was never your source of strength."[31]

We want to be very clear here: our view is that magick resides in all things, yourself included. You are powerful, but you do not wholly imbue all magick into an object you are using in your spellcasting. That object already has inherent magickal qualities in and of itself. What happens in witching is that you enhance your magickal energies with certain objects whose magickal energies correspond with your intent and align with you, specifically.

Just as Thor is not the god of hammers, you are not the witch of quartz or dragon's blood. Thor is the god of thunder—he harnesses an element, becomes one with it, and then manipulates that force to align with his will. You are a fire witch, a blood witch, water witch, kitchen witch, whatever—you're not an athame witch or an altar witch. You do not belong to a tool; it belongs to you. The tool does not make you a witch; rather, it is *you* as a witch who makes the tool.

....

31 *Thor: Ragnarok*, directed by Taika Waititi, written by Eric Pearson, Craig Kyle, Christopher L. Yost, October 10, 2017 by Marvel Studios.

EMPOWERMENT EXERCISE
Empower an Object with Your Intention

Find a stick, stone, crystal, or any tool you intend to use magickally. Sit with it in a quiet place and contemplate its purpose in your magickal practice. Consider why you have chosen this object. Think of how this tool may direct your focus when you are working with it.

Using the exercises in this chapter, identify your intention for this object and then declare (aloud or silently) that you will now imbue that intention into the tool. When you are ready, hold the item in your hands and speak to it. Start telling it what you intend for it to do. Then close your eyes and imagine your intention as a light that resides in your mind. You can use visualization, internal dialogue, or simply speak out loud what you are imagining. Say or picture that the light is growing, spreading through your body. Your intention suffuses all of you from the top of your head to the soles of your feet, the light moves out to cover every inch of your body. The light is your intention, and you are one with it.

Once you can see, feel, imagine, or verbalize that the light, the intention, is integrated into every aspect of you, begin to collect it into the center of your chest. You might describe aloud or visualize yourself gathering every bit of the intention light into one point that correlates with your heart. Focus on that one point and call out the intention, naming the light. Then begin to move the intention to your hands.

As the light enters your hands, exhale forcefully through your nose and flex your fingers around the object. Feel yourself pushing the light into the item. Speak out loud if you wish and tell the intention light that it now resides in that focus tool. You have now empowered the item with your intention.

The Intentions Are There

The power of writing intentions cannot be overstated, and you can hardly find a more inexpensive avenue to manifesting your desires. This process is empowered by your wisdom and intuition and animated by your will. You might have the writing of a two-year-old; that does not matter. The words could be spelled wrong, but the intentions are there. And that is all that matters.

Remember that this exercise is about your intentions and magick: manifestation is not dependent on whether you burn your spells or write them on a bay leaf. It does not matter if you are using a pen, pencil, or crayon. You could even use a piece of paper you found in the trash and a chalky rock from the side of the road—it is the energy of the intention itself that matters. The words you use and the process of capturing and pinning them down are the actions you take to launch your spell toward success.

As was said at the beginning of the chapter, intention completes a trifecta when partnered with intuition and wisdom. Unlike intuition and wisdom, intention bridges both the intangible and tangible realms. It is one of the most dualistically powerful and pliable aspects of how you communicate in both the magickal and mundane planes. The two-fold acts of combining your intuition, wisdom, and intention followed by loading a physical representation of your intention into each component of your spell creates concrete, tangible connections to those intentions. The result is magick that works.

THE
TANGIBLES

In this section you will learn to apply your intuition, wisdom, and intention in tangible ways. While part 1 focused on the more esoteric aspects of tapping into the intangibles related to a magickal practice of self-empowerment, this half focuses on seeing those principles in action through the acts of bringing them into the physical world. Foraging, finding, and fabricating share an interrelatedness in the same way that intuition, wisdom, and intention work together. Both triads—the physical and metaphysical—function independently and reciprocally in equal and powerful ways within their own domains. They send threads of connection across the physical and metaphysical spheres, reinforcing your magickal practice. Foraging, understanding and actively experiencing the world around you as your magickal warehouse, relates to intuition and wisdom, and finding, the ability to see and make connections between the various objects that have called to you, relates to intention and wisdom. Fabricating is the physical culmination of all three intangible aspects of Thrifty Witchery combined with the skills of both finding and foraging.

CHAPTER 5

Let's Get Practical

Many witches live in a world that inundates them with unrelenting messages about the supposed need to buy and own all the things. So often, social media presents us with images that seem to be designed specifically to increase our longing to obtain that perfectly cut and polished amethyst or that intricately carved wooden altar piece.

Paul Lawrence and Nitin Nohria, professors at Harvard Business School and authors of *Driven: How Human Nature Shapes Our Choices*, posit that humans possess four core drives that affect how we make our choices, the first of which is the drive to acquire, defined as: "the desire to obtain or collect physical objects, as well as immaterial qualities like status, power, and influence." They continue, making observations about the role of businesses: "[Those] built on the drive to acquire include retailers, investment brokerages, and political consulting companies. Companies that promise to make us wealthy, famous, influential, or powerful connect to this drive."[32]

Our witch's heart might swoon over the beautifully crafted, perfectly curated magickal items stunningly displayed in social media, and if we are fortunate enough to afford any of them, we may choose to make the acquisition, fulfilling our drive

....

32 Paul Lawrence and Nitin Nohria, *Driven: How Human Nature Shapes Our Choices* (Hoboken, NJ: Jossey-Bass Publishing, 2002), as quoted by Josh Kaufman, The Personal MBA blog, updated 2022, https://personalmba.com/core-human-drives/.

to acquire. Our decision to make that purchase might also be impacted by a fear of missing out, perhaps coupled with a fear that somehow our witchiness just does not quite measure up. But counterintuitively, when we submit to these fears what we are actually doing is causing ourselves to miss out.

As we are on the planet and *of* the planet, how we interact not only has a ripple effect on the rest of the ecosystem but also sends a crystal-clear message to every entity just what we think of them. To be a witch is to live in symbiosis with the energies surrounding you and in a way that values and honors your relationships with air, fire, water, earth, and spirit in all their myriad manifestations. The witchy way of living does not ascribe value to much you can buy or how on-trend your tools are but instead the degree of authenticity that exists in your relationships both with yourself and with each element.

Your surroundings are filled with energies that you interact with daily. An unseen sea of energies is already in relationship with you. From the dandelions in your yard to the oak tree near your apartment, you are surrounded by ingredients and tools that are already in tune with your energy signature to some extent. We will dive deeper into this in the chapter on foraging. In magickal terms, this energetic sea can be understood as a system within which the energy of each entity is shared and combined with the energies of all other entities. The human act of intentionally sharing and combining specific energies is what we call spellcasting.

Up to this point in the book, everything we have taught you has incurred no costs beyond your time and attentive energy. Your intuition, wisdom, and intention are all non-tangible assets that you already possess. Part 1 focused on identifying and strengthening these skills. Here in part 2, you will be using these freshly honed proficiencies to undergird your ability to forage, find, and fabricate your magickal tools. How?

Let's look at intuition, wisdom, and intention as they relate to foraging, finding, and fabricating. Yes, you may want all the things, but what does your intuition tell you that you need? An altar? A pentacle? A wand? (Hint: we both believe all you need is you.) The list of accoutrements can be overwhelmingly endless. But remember, you are building a magickal practice one component at a time.

Using the skills learned in the intuition chapter, open yourself up to what your higher self might be telling you about where to start first. What is the one thing that would make you feel more intimately connected to your magick? Is it an object or an activity? Is it a certain way of looking or a certain way of being?

How do the insights you have gleaned from your wisdom affect the decisions you make about setting priorities and budgeting? Yes, you may want to spend money on a magickal item but, in the larger context of your overall budget, would that purchase be wise? Shopping with intention—that is, sticking to your budget—can eliminate the financially flabby practice of impulse buying. This is not to say you can never make an impulsive purchase; rather, if you know that spur-of-the-moment buys are something you do, you can lean into your wisdom to budget for them.

To begin creating a budget, figure out your monthly income, deduct your standard monthly expenses (e.g., housing and utilities costs, food, transportation, etc.) and see if there is any money available after your expenses are met. If there is, set aside a very small percentage of the excess for possible impulse purchases for that month and be vigilant about not exceeding that designated amount no matter how tempted you may be. If by the end of the month you have not made any impulse purchases, roll the amount you saved into the next month's budget.

If there is not any monetary excess after meeting your monthly expenses, start thinking outside of the box: are there any items you have already budgeted for that can also be used for magickal purposes? Later on we talk about how some of the foodstuffs you may already be buying at the grocery can also be used in magick-making. We also offer you some very practical tips to reuse, recycle, repurpose, and refurbish items that you may not think could be remotely magickal—but with your intuition, wisdom, and intention you can transform what was once thought of as mundane into something filled with magickal purpose.

The first half of the book features Empowerment exercises; in this half you will find Practical practices such as the one below.

Practical Practice
DIY Tarot or Oracle Cards

You can make your own your tarot or oracle deck using card stock and pens (or pencil or crayons or paint), or computer-generated art. If you have a cell phone with a camera function, you can take photos that represent each card and then print them onto card stock, cutting individual cards to size. Oracle decks can have as many or as few cards as you decide and are almost unlimited in their imagery options.

What You'll Need

    White- or light-colored card stock (heavy-weight paper)

    Drawing tools/photos/images cut from magazines/
       computer-generated images

    Glue (optional)

    Scissors

    Paper (optional)

What You'll Do

Cut the card stock into rectangles, circles, or whatever shape you would like your cards to be. If you are drawing/painting your images, be sure to practice on a separate piece of paper before setting the final image onto your card. If you decide to use printed images, play around with them on the card to make sure the card reflects the message you want it to before gluing them into place.

Aside from the mechanics of card-making, creating your own personalized tarot or oracle deck offers you an ongoing opportunity to really meditate on and identify how you want to express aspects of your intuition, wisdom, and intention through the cards.

Possible Uses

    Divination

    Meditation

Putting Practicality to Work

Thrifty Witchery is all about seeing the world around you with a witch's eyes and a witch's mind. Because the magick is within you, you have the ability to change everything you touch into a tool that supports your magickal practice. In the chapters that follow, we will show you how to do just that.

You can choose to use the practices we share or simply store them away for a later date. Many of these are adaptable so feel free to change what works for you. Since no individual witch's magick is likely to look exactly like another's following these practices exactly as they are laid out may not be in the stars for you. Instead of attempting to mirror our spells, crafts, and creations, allow your own intuition, wisdom, and intentions to guide your work so that it is truly yours and no one else's.

CHAPTER 6

Foraging

There is a world of naturally occurring magickal items literally outside your doorstep. All any witch needs to do is get outside and begin exploring. The earth is ripe with offerings that can become powerful aspects of your magick. Bones, iron railroad spikes, river stones, herbs or other plant life, and more can be incorporated into your practice. You can do so much magick when the world becomes your apothecary, and you can do that magick without spending one red cent.

Venturing into the world with an open mind and an intentionally mindful connection to the experiences you have while foraging for your magickal tools can and often will garner dramatic results. Whether you end up trudging out of a forest with a haul of animal bones, moss, and sticks or you come home from an adventure in the city with a discarded piece of furniture found on the curb, the world always has magickal items to offer. You need only see these items' potential to fully equip yourself with whatever you have discerned as enhancements to your spellcasting.

What Is Foraging?

Most of us probably have a pretty good idea of what foraging is: the act of going out and searching for something we want or need. But let's take a few minutes to think about what the secondary effects of foraging can be when we dare to explore.

The foraging that wild animals do is a key component of maintaining their overall fitness and maintaining their fitness in turn has a positive impact on their ability to survive. Similarly, when witches forage for their magickal supplies, the overall hardiness of their magick increases. Why? Because the act of foraging brings you into a closer relationship with your environment, which in turn sharpens your ability to perceive subtleties. The more adept you are at perceiving subtleties and nuances, the more powerful your witchcraft becomes.

To be successful at foraging requires you to be familiar enough with the areas you are searching to notice whatever is standing out in it. If you are in a natural space, your awareness of what grows where and in which season directly affects the success of your hunting. Likewise, knowing which animals roam the natural areas around you or learning what kinds of soil or stones or shells are readily available increases your odds of finding something that will be just right for what you need.

Foraging is not just relegated to parks and recreation areas. If you are nowhere near a park or preserve or have no way to get to one, urban areas offer ample opportunities to increase your awareness of your surroundings. Knowing your area's bulk trash pick-up schedule or researching give-away events at local businesses is an important part of urban foraging, as is familiarizing yourself with local regulations about dumpster diving.

Foraging is not just about product—what you find—it is about process, too. How alert are you to the possibilities all around you when you look with a witch's eyes? How does your relationship with the world change when you see what is around you not simply in terms of assigned value or purpose, but also in terms of potential? How does what you think about the way things work change when you identify things in terms of how they might come together to manifest your desires?

Foraging serves to further ground us in our identities as witches, and the more grounded we are, the more powerful we become.

Foraging Your Magickal Tools

What image comes to mind when you think about foraging for your magickal tools? Is it perhaps the somewhat tired though delightfully compelling trope of the weathered crone living with her scraggly cat in a rustic wattle-and-daub cottage deep in an ancient coniferous forest. See as she takes her hand-woven wicker basket upon her arm and heads out to go wandering and witching for the day in search of the ingredients for her future decoctions. As she leaves the cottage, a crow lights upon her shoulder and a fox emerges from under the blackberry bushes to join crone and crow on their ramble. It is a pretty picture, isn't it? Your foraging adventures probably will not resemble this in the least, but they are no less magickal.

In addition to residing within you, magick can also be found in every plant growing everywhere. Whether they are house plants or the weeds in your yard, the sheer act of their climb toward the sun is not only a botanical function but also truly magickal as they feed off the sun's energy, the nourishment from the earth, hydration from water, and the procreative properties the wind provides.

Beyond the caveats of legally protected species, there are very few limits to what a witch can forage or gather in outdoor spaces. From the remains of roadkill to the discarded feather of a bird in flight to the fallen tree branches in the woods and the dandelions in your yard, magickal tools are everywhere.

In terms of botanicals, whatever we can find on the land we live on holds power not only because it exists in our environment but also because most of these plants are known to have magickal correspondences. Additionally, many herbs right outside your door can hold new and powerful meanings unique to you. Consider the dandelion: if you were to dig up the roots of one cluster of these sunny little pests, you would find that the root is thick, that it runs deep, and that it is the strongest part of the plant. Long, strong roots like this can be a powerful expression of magickal intention when incorporated into spells that address grounding, persistence, strength, and a host of other related traits that you may be trying to manifest.

A fallen branch found while hiking in the woods may appear to be simply a stick, but to a witch it has the potential to become a wand or an altarpiece or possibly fabricated with other sticks into a pentacle or some other shape. The only limit to the tools you might develop from your findings is your imagination. Later we will dive deeply into fabricating what we've foraged and found in our pursuit of magickal tools. For now, our focus is identifying the witch's tools in nature and the myriad ways we can responsibly harvest, adopt, and work with these items.

Caveats and Legalities

You must protect yourself and respect your environment in both your mundane and magickal lives. Both come into play when understanding legalities and caveats, particularly related to foraging for your magickal items. Specific laws are beyond our scope here; what follows is only a brief review of some of the more universal legal issues you may face when foraging.

Feathers

In the United States, it is illegal to collect (pick up and take) a feather from any of more than 800 species of migratory birds (Migratory Bird Treaty Act of 1918). These include feathers from barn owls, crows, cardinals, and many more birds whose energies witches and Pagans love to incorporate into their practices.

The only exemption is the Eagle Feather Law, which allows the collection of Bald Eagle and Golden Eagle feathers by Native Americans for religious purposes. Even if your practice is shaped by Native American beliefs, you cannot legally pick up and take an eagle feather you might be lucky enough to find on the ground unless you are an Indigenous person.

Does this mean if someone sees you picking up an owl feather or crow feathers that they are going to report you? It's very unlikely. In the end, how you choose to respond to this federal law is up to you. Nonmigratory and invasive bird species are not covered by the act, so feathers from birds such as turkeys, chickens, and doves are legal to collect and take home.

Trespassing

In the simplest terms, trespassing occurs when a person intentionally enters or remains on someone's property without authorization. Intent is the key concept; if you accidentally wander onto someone's land you are not criminally trespassing. If there are "No Trespassing" signs posted or if the property is fenced and you still enter, you are criminally trespassing and can be prosecuted. Many times, the result is an infraction or misdemeanor, but in some cases trespassing can be considered a felony.

Trespassing can also occur on public lands such as parks. If there are signs posted about the hours of operation—for example, from dawn until dusk—and you are on the property before or after the posted hours, you can be charged with trespassing, especially if you refuse to leave after being told to do so by the property owner or local authority. Please follow all laws when foraging, and if you are unsure about where you are wandering, do some research on the area before visiting or choose another location that you know is legally accessible.

Cemetery Laws

Every state has basic laws pertaining to cemeteries, though these laws may differ by state. Cemeteries are subject to the laws of ordinary property (like your house) as well as laws specific to designated burial properties. Generally, the two classifications of cemeteries are public (that is, you can buy burial plots) and private (restricted for use by people related to each other by blood or marriage). Remember, what is written here is a vast over-simplification of some very specific laws; you are strongly advised to conduct your own research before foraging for anything in a cemetery. As with other property, if you are on site before or after posted hours or if you access the cemetery after the gates have been closed, you are trespassing. Whatever your personal opinion about the law may be, choosing to trespass is an act that splashes disrespectful energies into any foraging you may do while there. If you decide you want to use graveyard dirt in your spellcasting, be selective and respectful. Try to use dirt from the grave of someone you knew in life whose energy in your life aligns with the spell you are planning to cast. Alternatively, you could use dirt from someone known to you but with whom you did not have a relationship. Remember too that you do not need a lot of dirt—a teaspoon will do. And it should go without saying but do not forage from mementos that have been left on any of the graves.

Health Warnings

Always exercise reasonable caution when foraging your materials. Be very careful with found items such as rusty nails, which can infect open wounds. As well, observe reasonable caution when collecting plant materials. Some plants are caustic and/or poisonous. If you are hunting mushrooms, for example, you will need to know which are safe for human consumption and which are poisonous. Arm yourself with a plant guide and a sturdy pair of gloves before foraging, and avoid skin contact with botanicals until you know for sure if they are safe for humans.

PRACTICAL PRACTICE
Rusty Nail Protection

The use of rusty nails for protection and warding has its roots in folk magick. They can be used to secure or pin down problematic situations and/or people, or to impede a problematic person's workings. Rusty nails have been included in witch bottles as one of the protective ingredients and are often ingredients in warding bags to protect against evil crossing the threshold(s) of a dwelling place.

What You'll Need

    Rusty iron or steel nails

    Bag to hang them in (optional)

    Something to pound them into the ground, such as a
       hammer (optional)

    Something representing the problematic issue or person
       (optional)

    Water (optional)

    Salt (optional)

    Hydrogen peroxide (optional)

    White vinegar (optional)

What You'll Do

If you do not have rusty nails, you can easily fabricate them one of two ways. The simplest method is to soak iron or steel nails in a solution of salt water for a few days or until they are as rusted as you need them to be. An alternate method is to make a rusting solution of white vinegar (2 ounces), hydrogen peroxide (16 ounces), and salt (2½ teaspoons), which will transform your nails a little more quickly.

After deciding how you are going to use your rusty nails, create an intention that will empower the nails to become the focus objects for the magick you will call into being using your intuition and wisdom. For example, if you are pinning down a problematic person, do this work either outside in an area that will be undisturbed or, if indoors, in a potted plant. Use a photo or drawing of the person. Concentrate on the image while speaking your intention into life. Then place the image faceup on the dirt. Take one (or as many as your intuition tells you is needed) of the rusty nails and pound it (or them) into the image and as deeply into the dirt as possible while speaking your intention to pin that person's energies in place so they can do no harm to you. If you do this in a potted plant, you may find it easier to pierce the image with the nail(s) first and then press the nail(s) and image into the potting soil until they are flush with the dirt. Do this using the palm of your dominant hand.

Adjust your intentions and spellwork accordingly if you plan to use the rusted nails in a protection bag—speak those intentions into life as you hang your protection bag(s) by the threshold(s) of your dwelling place.

Possible Uses
> Protection
> Binding
> Hexing

Intentions In Foraging

When a witch sets out in search of magickal tools in the natural world, be their destination a forest, desert, river, ocean, city, or any other landscape, they are tapping into three of the four aspects mentioned in the first half of this book. At the forefront of these witch traits is empowerment. The witch acknowledges that they could stumble upon what they need for their magickal processes.

Trudging along the city streets or mountain trails, a witch is keenly aware that what comes across their path is likely meant for them. They could come upon a discarded chest that may become their new curio cabinet, or they may simply find a stone in a riverbed. We want to specifically note that we are not advocating that you snatch up items that clearly belong to other people, such as items left behind on the neighborhood playground, for example. We are talking about objects that have clearly been abandoned or discarded. The magick of foraging is present in the knowing that discarded items or natural objects that have been found now belong to the witch. The magick is present in this situation because not only is the witch empowered, they have also intentionally developed the ability to heed their intuition and access their wisdom while foraging.

Foraging as a witch is not that different from the mundane foraging popular today among the many mycophiles hunting mushrooms in forests. The process is relatively similar: a mushroom hunter must know something about mushrooms, lest they collect the wrong ones, cook them up, and then poison themselves. In addition to being familiar with the names and types of fungus growing in shady, damp, wooded areas, these hunters must also have a sense for the most likely place to find their chicken of the woods or chanterelles.

Using wisdom and intuition in concert with each other is a witch's sweet spot when it comes to foraging. Some witches might set intentions while foraging their magickal tools, however this witch's skill is not necessary when being led by the Source to locate magickal items in the wild. In other words, one could set an intention to happen upon a rocking chair while foraging the local hills near their house. While finding a rocking chair in the hills is a possibility, it is highly unlikely. It is much more in alignment with the energies around you to set an intention for a rocking chair and see it come to fruition when seeking and finding such a thing in a furniture store or garage sale. This process of setting an intention to find a rocking chair aligns more to finding, which is covered in the next chapter.

Adventuring while empowered with your wisdom and intuition is a sure-fire way to explore the world and acquire the tools that will eventually build or enhance your practice. Understanding that the remains of animals, plant life, rocks, and even random sticks can all be used to feed your witch's power is a liberating idea that not only increases your proficiency in spellcasting but also allows you to let go of the idea that spending any amount of money is necessary in your magickal endeavors.

Adopting the Dead

The remains of the dead have power. Not only were they once living and breathing beings but, especially in the case of animals, these beings had a deep and meaningful connection to the world around them. When foraging for animal carcasses or other remains it is important to recognize how each animal interacts differently with their environment. Often their connection to the place in which they live is symbiotic.

Opossums scavenging in the forest near your house or in the trash in an apartment complex has the same goal regardless of where they are searching for food. They are there to eat what was discarded, and in doing so clean the organic filth of the world. They exist in a cycle of life that places them lower on the food chain and yet they are as essential as apex predators.

Every animal, no matter where they are, has its function. Whether it is a snake, goat, mountain lion, or human; every creature on this earth is present for a purpose. Why then should their purpose end just because their life has? Energetically speaking, finding a coyote skeleton while out walking could easily be a sign that it is your time to work with a little protection or even trickery.

Learning how to gather the bones, clean them, and honor the spirit of the dead while working with the energy they provide is essential when working in this realm of magick. Foraging for what once lived and bringing it into your sacred space can be a powerful act when coupled with your wisdom, intuition, and intention.

Cleromancy, or casting lots, is a form of divination written about in the Bible and that can be found in many different cultures throughout the history of the world.[33] It is thought to be a way to determine a deity's will. One popular choice for this form of divination are bones. Some of the more common items one may find in a cleromancy set is raccoon penis bone and chicken bones.[34]

Bones

Vincent used to refer to collecting bones as "harvesting" them. After a conversation with another witch, he has come to understand that the idea of adopting the spirit and bones of the animal is more respectful and more accurately describes the mindful approach he takes when doing this work. To harvest something is to cut it from the stalk, to store it, and to live off it. This cycle is more commonly associated with food grown in fields and farms. We harvest what nourishes and sustains us.

Working with the bones of a dead animal could easily align with a mindset of using what has been harvested, as the bones

....

33 Sandra Sweeny Silver, "Casting Lots in the Bible" Early Church History website, September 15, 2021, https://earlychurchhistory.org/beliefs-2/casting-lots-in-the -bible/.

34 Joanne O'Sullivan, *Book of Superstitious Stuff: Weird Happenings, Wacky Rites, Frightening Fears, Mysterious Myths & Other Bizarre Beliefs* (Watertown, MA: Charlesbridge Publishing, 2010), 87.

would very much be a magickal tool that both nourishes and sustains a magickal practice for the practitioner. However, to adopt something means entering a symbiotic relationship with it: you love it hopefully as much as it loves you. What one adopts is not simply maintained by the adoptee; there is an exchange of energy that feeds and empowers both parties. Adopting the carcass of an animal means you have upped your mindfulness, and that you will treat the bones with reverence, respect, and dignity. In return for your honor, they will provide an energetic exchange that honors you.

Every animal has different aspects of their natural disposition. An opossum or raccoon is typically a scavenger. They lurk in the dark hours and seek whatever remains in the discards that may be of value. The energy of these types of creatures may be used in magick to help the witch seek a new path forward, or in a frugal practice that empowers and uplifts their magick. Deer, on the other hand, graze. They move slowly across a field eating grass and greenery, all the while maintaining a hyper-awareness of their surroundings. They remain alert and ready to speed away from danger when they sense even the smallest movements. In this way, adopting the antlers or other bones of a deer can infuse a witch's magick with awareness, protection, and even speedy departures.

Gather Them Safely

When gathering animal remains, it is important to follow a few simple precautions to avoid illness. Animals can become sick, too, and it may not be clear what has caused a creature's death. There are plenty of reasons an animal may die; to assume a creature was healthy at the time of death is folly. Zoonotic disease is a very real threat, making any effort to protect yourself and your loved ones from this type of illness imperative.

Always wear protection when collecting the remains of a deceased animal. In an ideal world, a witch who forages for the dead would be prepared with items such as gloves, goggles, and containers for carrying carcasses. This is not always the case, however, as you might not expect to come across the remains of an animal when out and about. If this happens, it will serve you well to remember that if you touch dead things, *never* touch your face, orifices, or any open wounds until you can properly wash your hands. Again: if you are not able to secure the remains while wearing protection, clean your hands thoroughly afterward. Alternatively, you could forage for anything that would be suitable for carrying or containing the animal's body. A solution could present itself in the form of litter on the ground or even large leaves and sticks. When transporting the remains, keep maintaining sanitary practices. Always clean up after yourself so that there is no opportunity for potential diseases to contaminate any surfaces that you may come in contact with later.

It is best to be aware of local laws around foraging dead creatures, as there are not only protected animals but also laws regarding taxidermy. Take the time to research any specific laws before foraging in a location where you are likely to find animal remains.

Cleaning the Bones

There are several ways to clean the bones you are adopting, some of which can become costly. One common way is using *Dermestid maculatus* or hide beetles. These beetles are typically used for cleaning bones for taxidermy. Colonies of these types of beetles can be purchased; however, buying Dermestid beetles from less than reputable vendors always presents a risk. It is possible to receive beetles infested with mites that will ultimately kill the colony. The price range for a colony of beetles from a reputable place is typically between seventy and three hundred dollars depending on the size of the colony, which is neither frugal nor very thrifty. For that reason, what follows are two penny-wise ways to clean the meat from a set of bones.

Boiling the Bones

One of the ways a witch can clean the meat from the bones of animals they are adopting into their practice is to boil them in water. This is best done outside, if possible—it smells horrible. If you are processing the bones outside, it is best to build a small fire pit and use an old pot large enough to hold the animal parts. Set a grill over the fire so that your pot can rest on top of it. If you are processing the bones on your stove, you may want to open some windows to help dissipate the stench. Put the bones in the pot and fill with plenty of water. When your water boils, it may sometimes bubble over the rim of the pot; of course, water will evaporate as it boils. In either case, keep an eye on the pot and add water as needed. If you are working outside, continue to feed the fire. And no matter where you boil, be sure to check the meat on the bones to see if it has fallen off, which could take anywhere from two to ten hours depending on the state of decay and the size of the carcass. Be sure not to overdo it, however, because boiling a bone for too long could cause it to become damaged and ineffective as a tool. Boil until the meat has come off the bone, then remove the bones from the heat source and the water.

Bones are weak conductors of heat, so you will find that they cool quickly. After removing any excess meat from the bones, it is time to disinfect them. This process will ensure that there are no lingering bugs or potential sources of illness on the bones and is the same no matter which cleaning process was used.

Letting Nature Clean the Bones

The second and easiest way to clean the meat from your newly adopted bones is to let nature take its course. You do not need much at all to follow this process: Locate a place outdoors where you can secure the carcass on the ground. Dead and decaying things tend to smell, so keep in mind that for several days, you will not want the animal's body in a place where you could smell it.

Once you have the perfect location, place the dead body on the ground. One of the best places to perform this type of cleaning is over an ant hill, with which you are not only obtaining what you want—cleaned bones—but you are also feeding a colony of ants. This is an excellent way to live in symbiotic relationship with the natural beings around you. The only caveat to this is that when you collect the cleaned bones, you will have to deal with the ants.

It is very important to place the body in a container that cannot be moved by wildlife. If you have dogs or live in a rural setting, you are likely aware of what the animals in your local area can manage to move. Weighing down the covering is vital if you want to keep the bones where they are during the cleaning process. Using items such as pots or buckets to cover the carcass and then weighing the covering down with stones or bricks is ideal. Above all, it is most important to adapt to your natural environment and the pests or wildlife that you may deal with.

Once the bones are covered, simply wait. If you were to check on your bones in three days, you would find that maggots, ants, and other insects have taken over the body. After about a week, you will see progress on the removal of the meat. The amount of time this takes varies based on the sizes of the bones but typically should be complete in about two weeks.

No matter which method you used for clearing meat from the bones, collect them and then move on to sanitizing and disinfecting them.

Sanitization and Disinfection

To ensure your safety, take the time to sanitize your new bone allies. Place your bones in a freezer bag, seal it, and then set the bones in the back of your freezer. Leave the bones there for at least a week to kill any bugs that might be on them. After a week, pull the bag of bones out of the freezer and let them sit in the sealed bag for three days. A windowsill that receives full sun is the best location. After three days, place the bones back in the freezer for another week.

If there are any bugs remaining after this freezer cycle, they will be frozen and die. Setting the bones out for three days allows any eggs to hatch, but those little insects will not have the time to procreate before you freeze the bones again, making this a surefire way to eliminate any stubborn pests.

Your next step is to submerge the bones in peroxide. The peroxide will not only provide additional sanitation but also help to whiten them (if that is important to you). Pay close attention to the amount of time you leave them submerged—peroxide causes the bones to become brittle and could cause them to decompose if left for too long. Keep the bones in the peroxide no longer than twenty-four hours.

Once you remove the bones from the peroxide rinse them in tap water so there is no residual peroxide as it could continue to break down the bones.

Let the bones dry and then use them later for anything from divination to altar pieces or other witchy tools. Fabricating any finds into tools is covered in a later chapter.

Honoring the Sacrifice

After you have foraged, cleaned, and adopted the bones of the dead, you must honor the sacrifice of the animal you will work with. This can look as many ways as there are humans on the earth. The key point is to express gratitude that the remains found their way to you. Never disrespect any sort of energy or spirit you plan to work with as this could create a disconnect between you and the magick you create.

When honoring your adopted animal remains, take the time to clear them of any dust that accumulates, talk to them as if they are friends, and give them spaces that are theirs both when in use and when stored for a later purpose.

In fact, it is essential that you care for all your magickal items with the same level of concern that you would for yourself or your loved ones. Never neglect your bones or any other magickal tool in your possession. Doing so is sure to result in a multitude of issues from spell backfires to an inability to manifest your desires.

PRACTICAL PRACTICE
Bone Divination

Bone divination, or osteomancy, relies strongly on your ability to access and follow your intuition. The practice is centuries old and can be found across several cultures throughout the world. You can fabricate your own kit from cleaned chicken bones or, if you share your living space with wildlife, you can collect any bones you come across. You could even include shells, which are the "bones" of the sea, and bark, the "bones" of trees.

What You'll Need
    Clean, dry animal bones
    Seashells (optional)
    Bark (optional)
    Cloth or board to cast bones upon (optional)
    Container for bone set (basket or cloth bag)

What You'll Do
When selecting the bones you would like to include in your set, give thanks for the animal's life. Spend time handling each clean and sanitized bone mindfully as part of getting to know how it might be used in your divination. Trace your fingers along each bone's surfaces. Inhale the scents. Note the colorations and idiosyncrasies of each bone's textures. If you are comfortable doing so, give the bones a small lick. As you are getting to know your bones, allow your intuition and wisdom to guide you as you discern possible meanings for each bone. Wings or legs, for example, could pertain to journeys

or escapes (flight). Backbones could hold meanings related to burdens or bravery. If you have chosen to use seashells and/or tree bark, use the same process to familiarize yourself with them. Murex shells and other shells with round openings, for example, are favored by hermit crabs. In osteomancy, these shells can align with the concepts of growth or moving house, since hermit crabs leave their old shell when they have outgrown it and search for a larger one to inhabit. The claws of crabs can align with defenses or grasping what is desired. The patterns in tree bark as well as the species of tree the bark is from carry their own meanings.

The mechanics of osteomancy are straightforward: the querent forms a question, and then the diviner and the querent hold the question foremost in their minds as the bone set is shaken in its container or in the diviner's cupped hands. When the diviner intuits that the bones are ready to be read the bones are cast or gently tossed onto a flat surface to fall as they will. The diviner then reads the patterns the bones have made.

Possible Uses
   Divination
   Discernment

Plant Life

There is a consistent idea presented in social media and many books on witchcraft that seems to reinforce the belief that herbs and plant life are must-have components of successful spellcasting. While this is not actually the case, herbs and plants can be helpful, should you choose to incorporate them into your magick. Most metaphysical shops sell herbs that are commonly used in spellcasting, and many books (including this one) offer a plant usage list. However, herbs are not a magickal requirement, nor do they not have to be purchased; instead, you can forage for them.

Foraging for your own plant allies can be both magickal and empowering, as the act itself allows you to connect to what is being collected. The most amazing effect this can have on your magickal aptitude is that while foraging for plants, you could gain a new insight on how to use something that grows near you. This means that the moss you find on a rock could have a unique purpose for you other than the traditional properties of luck, money, or protection. For example, if you locate your own moss in the shadows, you might gain a sudden insight (intuition) that it can be a useful ally in your own shadow work. This is quite literally the magick inherent in foraging your own plant materials. Not only are you collecting what you need and infusing your energy into the botanicals from the very beginning, but you are also defining how and why you will use it.

When foraging for magickal plant allies, be aware of whether pesticides have been used where you have chosen to forage. Dandelions, for example, are commonly used in spellcrafting because of their solar energies and associations. However, in most of the public places where they are abundant—soccer fields, parks, roadsides—the dandelions have been treated with poison because the overculture perceives them to be unsightly weeds. Thanks to persistent public education campaigns, there is a growing awareness that dandelions are also an early spring food source for bees and as such should be left to grow untreated by pesticides. Even still, there is a pretty strong chance that dandelions you might collect from public spaces have been chemically treated; even if they have not, any areas that have been routinely treated with chemicals over the years are generally best avoided for harvesting. Instead, forage in places you know have not been treated with pesticides. If it is on private property, always ask the owner's permission first.

Know What You Are Collecting

In *The Witch's Path*, Thorn Mooney, High Priestess of a traditional Gardnerian coven in the American South, offers a multistep practice for building a devotional practice to the land. One of her suggestions is to learn "what natural resources have been historically harvested" in your area and what is currently being farmed or produced.[35] She also suggests that readers learn about what species of plants are native and whether they are edible.

Part of knowing what you are collecting may involve differentiating between native and non-native plants. Generally, plants considered native are only those that are indigenous to an area; that is, people did not introduce the plant into the environment at some point in history. How you plan to use the plant and what you are designing your spell to accomplish will inform the selections you make when foraging and considering native versus non-native species. Even if that is not crucial to your practice, you are still adding to your knowledge base, and *that* will give you a larger repository from which to draw.

....

35 Thorn Mooney, *The Witch's Path: Advancing Your Craft at Every Level* (Woodbury, MN: Llewellyn Publications, 2021), 74–75.

Drying Herbs

Wherever you gather your herbs from, they will probably need to be fully dried before they can be put to magickal use. Back in the day, herbs had to be hung to dry for several days prior to using in a spell, and many witches still prefer this time-honored method today. But sometimes a busy witch might want to take advantage of the advances in technology that dry herbs in a fraction of the time.

If you have one, an oven is one such option. Drying your herbs in an oven is pretty simple: set your oven on its lowest setting and then lay out the herbs you want to dry on a baking sheet. Store-bought fresh herbs are always food-grade quality, so you can use the same baking sheet you would use to cook meals. If your herbs have been harvested from outdoors, thoroughly clean them first to rid them of most of the pesticides and other pollutants that might be on them. Then use either a baking sheet that will never touch your edibles or a baking sheet lined with foil so that the herbs do not touch its surface.

Once the herbs are laid out the baking sheet and the oven has reached 175 °F (79 °C), slide the baking sheet into the oven and close the door. Set a timer for about five minutes and check the ingredients when the timer goes off. If the herbs are not dry, reset the timer and continue to check them every five minutes until they are crisp and crumble easily.

In the fabricating chapter are several projects that incorporate both dried and fresh herbs, as well as projects for other natural items you may discover while foraging for your magickal tools.

Sticks and Stones

Bones, herbs, and plants can be foraged, found, and processed in preparation for fabricating your magickal tools, and they can be combined in almost an infinite number of ways to support the magick you choose to manifest. Other items witches often forage for are rocks, crystals, and wood to use in their practice.

Chances are good that as a child you may have squatted in the dirt and drawn patterns in the dust with a stick, or maybe you collected pretty rocks you saw while were playing outside, stuffing them in your pockets to take home with you. What was it that attracted you to a particular stone or a specific stick? And what would happen to your magick-making if you invite the wisdom that you had as a child into your adult decision-making? Educational specialist Julia Gorham notes that

> as young children struggle to create a desired effect with a toy, they discover that it isn't always easy. They realize that there is perhaps a problem to be solved and that they have to practice acquiring and improve the skills necessary to achieve their goal.[36]

Magickal problem-solving, approaching sticks and stones with a child's curiosity and a child's wisdom, will give you the confidence to see the potential in whatever has caught your attention. It allows you to trust your intuition even if the message has not quite filtered to your adult brain yet. It lets you play with your magick and, in playing, to find out more about

....

36 Julia Gorham, "The Value of Play for Young Children" Montessori Rocks website, October 26, 2017, https://montessorirocks.org/value-of-play-for-young-children/.

how your personal magick works. Sticks and stones build up your magickal bones so spells will always serve you.

Crystals versus Rocks

What is the difference between crystals and rocks? In geological terms, a rock is what you get when two or more minerals clump together into a single organic solid. A crystal is a mineral that is not part of a cluster of other minerals and has a crystalline form.[37]

Crystals are just as compelling and powerful as the rocks that catch your attention as you are going about your day. It might sound like anthropomorphizing to speak in terms of building relationships with rocks, but if you think about it, aren't rocks earth itself? They are formed by intense pressures deep inside the earth, so in a very real sense when you are holding a rock in your hand, you are holding a part of the earth's heart.

When a rock catches your attention—when it reaches out to you, initiating contact—consider approaching it with your child's wisdom and your witch's intuition. Why might it be calling to you? What were you thinking about when you suddenly noticed it? How could its energies align with your own? How does the weight of it feel in your hand? When you stroke its surface, what do you notice? What are the potentials that might be manifested when working with this rock?

When we stop looking at rocks as earth's cast-offs and instead honor them as pieces of the earth's heart, the way we view the world around us undergoes a profound change. We

....

37 John, "Rock, Mineral, or Crystal? What's the Difference?" *How to Find Rocks* (blog), August 14, 2019, https://howtofindrocks.com/difference-between-rocks-minerals -and-crystals/#1-what-is-a-mineral.

begin to realize that there is really very little difference between the magickal and the mundane. It is all in how you look at it, and how you choose to act upon wisdom you have gained by seeing the world through a witch's eyes.

Wands and Walking Sticks

Like stones, wands can enhance your spellcasting. While many witches use them, just as many do not; it is up to you to discern if using a wand aligns with your magickal signature. A traditional wood for wands is oak with its long-held associations of power, justice, wisdom, and fertility. Oak trees grow everywhere, including near coastal regions, and there is every chance that some are growing in your environment.

PRACTICAL PRACTICE
Branch Wand or Staff

Crafting your own wand or staff from a branch that may have called to you on one of your foraging adventures can be immensely satisfying and empowering. Branches are not relegated to wooded areas; you may just as easily discover a piece of driftwood alongside a body of water that your intuition tells you would be the perfect wand or staff, as unique as you and your magick are. The same is true for densely urbanized areas; after strong storms or stiff winds, all kinds of branches may be readily available, waiting for you to notice them and take them home. Hiking trails are great places to forage for small branches but you do not have to be out in the semi-wilderness to find a potential wand. Look around outside after a strong thunderstorm to see if any of the small branches that have fallen might work for you. If you live in a neighborhood where the homeowners hire tree trimmers, wait until the crew has cleared the worksite and check the piles they have left out by the curb before bulk trash comes to pick the branches up.

What You'll Need
Branch, driftwood, or another wooden shaft

Light sanding paper (optional)

Cooking oil (optional)

Paper towels (optional)

Crystal, acorn, or another item to form a wand tip (optional)

Glue or other binding material to adhere wand tip and/ or staff decorations (optional)

Clamp to hold glued items together while drying (optional)

Ribbons, bells, charms, crystals etc. to decorate staff (optional)

What You'll Do
Whether you are crafting a wand or a staff, start by cleaning your branch of any loose pieces such as bark, cobwebs, old seed casings, and any other detritus. You are not stripping off the bark so much as making sure all the bark on the branch is firmly attached to the branch. If possible, do this outside; if you are working inside try to spread something such as a sheet under you for easy clean-up after you have cleaned your branch. You may want to lightly sand your branch after cleaning it simply to smooth over surfaces that are a little too rough. After sanding, use a paper towel or a cloth to remove any lingering dust. You

may want to rub a little cooking oil (such as olive oil) into the surfaces of your branch after sanding.

If you feel like decorating your wand or staff, your options are almost limitless: you can use old ribbons and yarns, bits of broken jewelry, or stones for a staff. If you choose to add a tip to your wand, you can add items such as acorns, crystals or stones, or even a twig pentacle. Tap into your intuition and let it come out to play!

Possible Uses
> Spellwork
> Raising and taking down energetic circles
> Drawing in energy
> Sending out energy

Urban Foraging

When foraging, how do you know when you have found something that is potentially useful? In the next chapter, we will cover setting an intention to find specific items in the next chapter. While foraging, you are not so much setting an intention that you will find a particular item as you are opening yourself to whatever you may happen upon, and finding happens in that moment when an object has caught your attention. Sometimes an item calls to you even when you are not actively foraging. When you train yourself to see the world with a witch's eyes, these seemingly random occurrences become not so much happenstance as they are the result of your subconscious mind being alert to the energies that are constantly percolating around you. After finding something that may align with your magickal practice, there are usually a few moments of examination during which you and the object tentatively explore whether you are a good energetic fit for each other. This magickal examination requires your wisdom and intention, using the wisdom you have accumulated to connect not only to the object, but to connect the object to one or more specific intentions.

The rusted iron nails you are sure to find in places such as garages or tool sheds can be used for protection or hexing. One old folk magick protection spell calls for marking out the four cardinal points on your property, pounding a rusty nail or rail spike into the soil, and speaking your protection spell while doing so. If you happen to live in or near horse country, keep an eye out for old, used, iron horseshoes, which have been used as luck charms for centuries and are an easy ward to place over or next to doorways and other entrances.[38]

Another tool shed find are washers, small flat circular metal discs with a hole in the middle. They can be strung up with whatever yarn or string you have on hand to a sturdy stick, creating a simple wind chime that you can hang outside, perhaps even decorating the east corner of your altar to represent the element of air. Wind chimes are thought to be good luck in parts of Asia, and in ancient Rome wind chimes (bells) were thought to keep evil spirits away.

Maybe you do not have a garage or a tool shed but have a friend or family member who does. Offer to help them the next time they are cleaning it out and ask if you can keep anything they plan to discard. Not only will you be helping your friend or, even better, doing something charitable, you will be reusing and recycling something that might otherwise end up in a landfill.

....

38 "The Legend of the Horseshoe," *Kentucky Derby Museum* website, March 11, 2014, https://www.derbymuseum.org/Blog/Article/52/The-Legend-of-the -Horseshoe.

And do not forget about the closets, basements, and attics of your friends and family, in addition to your own. Whether they are doing a spring cleaning or prepping for a garage or yard sale, offer to help. When you or they have finished sorting the piles of what to keep and what to trash, ask if you can go through the trash pile before bulk waste picks everything up. Do you live near a college or university? Cruise around the campus at the end of the semester to see what the dorm students have left out on the curb.

Check out area swap meets, which work strictly on a barter system. People bring usable items that they no longer need and trade them for things other people have brought to the meet. No money is exchanged, only objects or services. If you cannot find one near you, organize a meetup with friends or family. Again, not only are you reducing your carbon footprint; these acts help create and strengthen your community. In a very real sense, you are using your practical magick in adaptive and creative ways that change the world around you.

Dumpster diving is another viable option for foraging, but be sure to do research and check out the laws in your area. Many times dumpster diving is legal, but you need to be mindful about signage that warns against trespassing, littering, and vandalism. Dumpsters near storage rental units can be a goldmine. Respect any locked dumpsters and move on to the next potentially unlocked one and remember to dress appropriately (not in your favorite clothes) and use a sturdy pair of gloves.

If you are foraging outdoors, most cities maintain at least a few open-air recreational areas—parks or nature preserves are the most common—in which all sorts of useful tools and treasures may be foraged. Pentacles, for instance, can be fashioned from the twigs or small branches that can be found under and around trees (note: never remove healthy branches from living trees!). After arranging your twigs, you can affix them using glue, yarn, twine, thread, long blades of grass—whatever you have on hand.

PRACTICAL PRACTICE
Washer Wind Chimes

Wind chimes have been around since about 3000 BCE. Some people believe they attract the fae, others believe that they attract good luck, and still others believe the sounds of the chiming serve as a ward against evil spirits. Many others simply enjoy the sounds wind chimes make. Witches can use windchimes to represent east for outdoor altars or to honor wind energies.

What You'll Need
    Straight stick long enough to hang several washers from
    Flat metal washers (e.g., from a hardware or home
        improvement store)
    String, yarn, twine, or other material
    Colored markers (optional)
    Glue (optional)

What You'll Do
Make sure the stick is sturdy enough to support the washers you'll be hanging from it. Tie one end of the string to the stick and the other end to a washer. You want the lengths of string to be long enough that the washers can sway freely in the wind. Repeat this until you have several washers hanging at

intervals from the stick; you want them to have some distance from each other but not so much distance that they won't be able to brush up against each other when they catch a breeze. If you'd like, you can make sure the strings stay in place by adding a little glue to where you've knotted them on the branch. You can also use colored markers to add hues to the metal washers, if desired.

Possible Uses
> Attract the fae
> Marking the east quadrant of an outdoor altar
> Honor wind energies

The Unnatural Has Power Too

Found objects can hold great amounts of power, should you decide to align your energies with theirs. Consider the crow: these creatures are known for finding and collecting shiny objects. To our avian friends, these treasures may hold untold value even though to us it may just look like pieces of tinfoil. You never know what you might find walking down the street or wandering a hiking trail or along the beach. Like the crow, not everything you may find will be natural, but that does not necessarily mean that discarded objects are without value for use in your magickal practice. Keep your eyes peeled for random items that may serve as new altar pieces or even offerings that can be left for your deities.

One example is beach glass (found alongside fresh water sources such as lakes and rivers) and sea glass (found at saltwater beaches). Neither of these glasses occur naturally in their environments, yet when they coupled with your intuition and wisdom and brought to life by your intention, they can give a powerful boost to your magick-making. Things like old fishing nets that have been left behind or bits of rope or string can be taken home, washed, and used in witchy decor or in future knot spells.

Do not shy away from using recycled or upcycled plastic simply because it is a synthetic product. When cleaned and washed, those discarded multi-pack plastic yogurt or apple-sauce cups can be filled with soil and transformed into seedling trays for your magickal herb garden. These are just some of the tools that are already all around you, waiting for you to magick them into powerful implements.

PRACTICAL PRACTICE
Horseshoe Luck

The use of horseshoes for luck has its genesis in Irish folklore. The story goes that St. Dunstan, a blacksmith at the time, was visited by the devil, who asked that St. Dunstan make him a horseshoe. The blacksmith did and secured a red-hot horseshoe with iron nails to the devil's hoof. In excruciating pain, the devil begged St. Dunstan to remove the shoe, which he did after extracting a promise from the devil that he would always thereafter respect the horseshoe as a protection against him.

What You'll Need
    Horseshoe(s)
    Nail(s) (optional)

What You'll Do

Hang the horseshoe above the doorway(s) into your dwelling place. Some people hang them open-end up to catch luck, while others hang them open-end down so that luck pours down upon them. Use your intuition to discern which direction will work best with your energies. If you do not want to hammer the horseshoe in place, placing it on the ground by the side of the threshold works just as well. When affixing or setting your horseshoe into place, speak your intentions for the focus object.

Possible Uses

Luck

Protection

You Never Know What You Might Come Across

Foraging is about seeing what is already around you with keenness and a mind that is open to prospects. It is a way of retraining your brain to see potential connections and possible ways different components might creatively interconnect to enhance your magickal practices. Training your brain to see the objects of the world in terms of their interrelatedness in turn makes it easier to perceive all the myriad ways that unseen energies are also connected. Foraging also actively engages your wisdom and intuition in that when you are foraging you are actively using two of the three metaphysical cornerstones of powerful witchery.

In foraging it is always best to keep in mind that you do not know what you may come across. It is safe to say that the exploration of any environment could provide you with new magickal items. Always remain aware and do your best to respect both the laws of the land and the living creatures who may have benefited from the items you have taken as your own.

While being a witch does not require that you forage at all, doing so will enhance your practice exponentially and will create a stronger connection to the tools you acquire.

Foraging Quick-Pops

Start looking at the world as a ready-made apothecary shop and you'll start seeing resources all around you. To get started, here is a very brief sampling of what you might expect to find in some familiar places.

Public Parks, Beaches, Hiking Trails, and Other Non-Urban Spaces

Fallen branches of all sizes

Pinecones

Acorns

Seashells

Sea glass

Driftwood

Seaweed

A wide range of rocks

Sea, river, and/or lake water

Fallen leaves

Herbs and plants

Sweet gum tree balls

Animal parts (e.g., fur, scales, teeth, bones, or shed snakeskin)

Cities and Other Urban Areas

Garage sales, yard sales, and estate sales can be goldmines for decorative items such as:

Old beads

Old or broken jewelry

Used candles

Old crockery

Fabrics

Second-hand Halloween décor that can be repurposed in your practice

Church jumble or rummage sales often have several families participating, which make them worthwhile places to forage all kinds of items from fabrics to paints to glassware that can be used in ritual. If you see a store is going out of business, wait until the inventory is being offered for 75 to 90 percent off of the suggested retail price—even if the store has nothing remotely to do with witchcraft, you may still find something useful from which you can fabricate a witchy tool or accoutrement. Do not look at the merchandise in terms of what it is *intended* to do—look at it in terms of what *you intend* to do with it.

CHAPTER 7
Finding

In the same way that foraging is an act of combined wisdom and intuition, finding is a combination of intention and wisdom. When you have determined exactly what it is you need and you know precisely where to find it, you are no longer foraging; you are finding. Remember, foraging involves being wide open during your rambles to anything you might happen to come across that could be fabricated into a useful witchy item. Finding is a more streamlined process in which you seek out and find exactly what you are after, like when running to the grocery store for a specific herb or food item you have determined will be useful for your work, or setting out to explore your local thrift shops and garage sales for furniture, fabrics, or other items you have decided to incorporate into your practice. While most of this book is designed to help a witch formulate a magickal practice without spending any money, finding is likely the one area where you may incur a monetary cost of some sort in some way.

To be clear, finding is not simply about having a need that can only be fulfilled by spending some money; this is not the case at all. The reality is that when actively trying to find witchy tools or supplies, it's common to end up spending a tiny bit to acquire items such as string, candles, wax, fabric, paint, and so on. So, while in this chapter we do cover items you may need or want to purchase as you expand your magickal practice, the underlying theme remains firmly rooted in the four R's: Reuse, Recycle, Repurpose, and Reduce.

How Is Finding Different from Foraging?

Finding comes from knowing what you need and going out into the world to locate it. Foraging is more centered around happening upon items while out and about without an expectation that you will find a specific, predetermined object. Finding is all about making a clear decision about exactly what you are after and then seeking it in the most likely places. Like foraging, finding can occur just about anywhere. You may know that you need hardware such as screws, nuts, or wood; your next step is to go out to the shed, garage, hardware store or anywhere else you know you will find your needed items, a precise act of intention. When finding magickal tools and supplies, it is most often the case that we know exactly what we are looking for and exactly where we are most likely to find it.

To know what you need and where you can locate it is not just helpful, it is empowering. It feels good to know what you need, and it is affirming to have a goal that you know you can accomplish. The rush of endorphins—those "feel-good" hormones your central nervous system releases when you activate your internal reward system—once you have succeeded in finding exactly what you set out to find is incredibly satisfying. Finding just the right thing can be a very fulfilling part of your magickal practice. Although both foraging and fabricating (covered in the next chapter) can be as rewarding as finding, there is something about wisdom and intention working together in concert to buttress your ability to identify and find what you need that is intensely gratifying. When finding is a component of your practice, you almost always have an "aha!" moment when you get to say, "Yes! This is exactly the thing I was looking for and it is perfect."

Finding also has nuance to it: you may not always have a hyper-specific object in mind when finding but instead just an idea that comes into sharper focus as you dig into your wisdom about where you can find the item you seek. For example, let's say you know you need little glass jars. You might scour the internet or your local hobby shop in search of these bottles, but you could also choose to dig through the recycling bin to find the perfect little vessel.

In the end, what finding boils down to is knowing what you need and where to locate it. You might go to the oak tree in your front yard or the park because all you need is a twig or an acorn; you might need mint and the place you will find it is your garden or the grocery store. The crucial difference between foraging and finding is that you are not out looking until your intuition tells you that something is meant for you; instead, you are out seeking a specific item in a place where you know it is likely to be found.

Finding What You Already Have

Most of us have a treasure trove of items that are not being used. Maybe it is a junk drawer filled with rubber bands, pens, tape, pennies, and who knows what else. It might be a collection of randomness tucked away in your closet near the back where no one will ever see, piled high and full of items you were not ready to get rid of but you have no practical use for: a cardboard box, one old shoe, that broken belt you thought went with everything. You could even have a shelf stacked high with half-filled notebooks or art supplies you have not used in a decade, the sum total equating to broken crayons, dried paint, stiff brushes, and maybe even string or glitter. All of this stuff has potential. None of it needs to go to waste.

The "junk" you own can be repurposed. Many of us have all sorts of practical items that can be used to enhance a magickal practice. Bits of broken jewelry, old makeup, stubs of colorful street chalk, stained and/or worn clothing, and of course pantry items are just a few examples of household finds that, with the application of your wisdom and intention, can be used as powerful magickal allies. A bonus is that repurposed household objects are often already saturated with your energetic signature.

The first step in finding what you already have is to take a comprehensive inventory of what is taking up unnecessary space. Japanese organizing consultant Marie Kondo is known for her rule that if something does not spark joy, you should get rid of it. We would change this idea slightly: it is likely that some of what does not currently spark joy for you may be the means to create joy as components of your future magickal items. This is not to say that you should hold on to everything, (you don't want to star in the witchiest episode of *Hoarders* ever)—but you should take the time to identify what you need in your witchy life first and then begin cleaning out your spaces with the intention that you will find those things in the junk drawer, closet, or shelves, or stored in the back of the closet, in the attic, basement, or shed along with all the other seemingly useless things.

For example, you might need a bag to hold your tarot cards or a fire-safe surface for burning candles and incense. Or maybe you want to start a new spellbook. With these intentions in place, you can go through your scattered, unused belongings and begin to identify which of these things can be repurposed for such projects. Do not worry about fabricating things just yet; that comes later. For now, spend time finding the stuff you need in the junk you have.

Herbs, Oils, Spices, and More

Many times, you can find materials in your own kitchen that can serve your magickal purposes. Why not actively find what is already in your cupboard and then use your finds for spellcrafting or deity offerings? Exploring what you already have in your house and then identifying how you can use it in your spellcrafting is just as valid a way to work your magick as going to a witchy shop and buying herbs. Often you will find that the same herbs that can be bought in these more witchy environments cost less in non-witchy stores.

Pantry staples such as salt are commonly used in magick. You do not need to have sea salt to set a boundary or create black salt—any salt will work. Whatever you use for cooking oil can also be used to make infused herbal oils. You do not have to buy the best, fanciest olive oil to make an infusion when the vegetable oil you use to fry your chicken is already in your pantry. All kinds of fruits are sacred to multiple deities, and some deities even prefer leftovers as opposed to fresh food. Additionally, dumb supper plates or ancestor offerings do not need to be overflowing with food; a simple, small portion of what you have already cooked for yourself or your family is sufficient.

Eggs can be used in divination, protection magick, and cleansings. Honey is an all-purpose offering that can be used for just about any deity from Hindu to ancient Greek pantheons and many in between. Water is considered to be a purification element in almost every spiritual practice. From baths to crystal cleansings and even moon water, there is very little that cannot be worked with a cup of plain tap water. If all you have is water, be aware that it is always an appropriate offering not only across just about every pantheon but to the earth as well.

PRACTICAL PRACTICE
Black Salt

Black salt can be used in banishing spellwork and as a protective barrier against negative energies. It can also be used in lieu of hot-foot powder. Naturally occurring black salt comes from India and places where other Himalayan salt mines are located, such as Bangladesh and Nepal. You can fabricate your own using a couple of common ingredients in a few simple steps.

What You'll Need

> Sea salt (if available; otherwise, plain table salt is fine)
> Ash, such as can be found in a fire pit
> or
> Finely ground black pepper
> or
> Finely ground black chalk

What You'll Do

Formulate and speak your intention into the ingredients as you blend them. Use a ratio of ingredients that produces the degree of blackness you want. For darker salt, use more ash, black pepper, or black chalk than salt. Store your black salt in an air-tight container.

Possible Uses
  Banishing
  Protection

PRACTICAL PRACTICE
Eggshell Protection

In many folk magick practices, eggshells are ground up into a powder that is spread across thresholds, windowsills, and other openings to protect against negative energies and energetic beings. The idea is that the eggshell protects in powdered form the same way it protects the developing chick when whole. Finely-ground eggshells can also be added to bath water as part of a ritual purification. As with all spells, access your intuition and wisdom to create a clearly stated, concise intention to charge your eggshell powder.

What You'll Need
  Water
  Saucepan
  Stove or other heat source
  Eggshells, clean and rinsed
  Paper towels
  Sheet pan or other baking pan
  Liner for sheet pan (parchment paper or foil)
  Oven
  Food processor (or electric coffee grinder or rolling pin)
  Resealable plastic bags
  Flat workspace (kitchen counter is just fine)

What You'll Do

Bring water in a saucepan to boil, add eggshells and boil for 10 minutes. Drain and place eggshells on paper towels to fully dry for several hours (or overnight). When they are completely dry, place the eggshells on a sheet pan lined with parchment paper or foil and bake them in a preheated oven set to low (200 °F/93 °C) for about 10 minutes or until you can no longer see any moisture on them. Remove from the oven and allow to cool. Pulverize the eggshells using either an electric appliance or by placing them in a resealable plastic bag and bashing them with a rolling pin. Store the powdered eggshells in a fresh resealable plastic bag.

Possible Uses

>   Protective wards
>   Sigils
>   Purification

Finding in a Food Desert

Even if you live in a food desert (lacking good access to supermarkets or grocery stores) or consume mostly fast food and take-out, there are still opportunities to find magickal ingredients without having to set aside additional funds to support your witchiness. Just about every fast-food restaurant offers a variety of condiments that can be incorporated into your magick. You can ask for extra salt and pepper packets with your meal and save them for later magickal endeavors. You can use this salt to cast circles of protection, make salt water for cleansing some of your tools, sprinkle it on window frames or doorways, and even to create black salt.

Pepper packets can be saved to make all sorts of spells. Pepper is a common ingredient in hot-foot powder and is typically used in other banishing spells. Similarly, you can ask for extra honey packets with your fast-food breakfast sandwich. Save them for sweetening spells. When ordering your regular cup of morning beverage at the corner café, ask for or pick up some extra sugar packets; these can also be used in sweetening spells. If you are grabbing lunch from any Mexican food drive-throughs, ask for extra hot sauce packets—these can be incorporated into your spellwork for not only banishing but also speeding up magickal results.

Remember, you do not need to be greedy and snatch up a double-handful of packets; one or two extras will be more than sufficient for use in your spellcrafting. You do not need jugs of honey or quarts of sweet water to craft meaningful and powerful spells. Small containers with only a small amount of ingredients will work just as well as huge quantities of stuff for any spellcrafting. Magick was never and still is not about profligacy—it is and always will be about using what is on hand when you need it.

In Thrifty Witchery, what you use in your magick should reflect the items you already find in your life. This precept of practicality has wide and deep historic roots in folk magick practices used around the world. All too often modern witches are led to believe that if we do not have this item or that ingredient we will miss the magickal mark. This leads to a toxic and fear-based mentality that can only negatively affect the outcomes of your magick. Freeing yourself from the ideas that you must have a particular item or that you need specific amounts of supplies is liberating. Remember what we said in the first chapter: you do not have to keep up with or compete with any other witch's way of doing anything to be a powerful, power-filled practitioner. You already have everything you need to develop your witchery inside of you.

It cannot be said enough: *you* assign the purpose for the items and ingredients you are using. You are the be-all and end-all of your own practice, and you need only to train your witchy senses to see what is readily available and use your wisdom and intuition to practice and create magick that will work for you.

Frugality in magick is essential when practicing on a budget. Self-empowered magick is not about going beyond your means to accomplish your goals. We have shared just a few examples of the ways in which you can keep your existing spending habits intact while acquiring magickal items for use in spellwork. Creativity is the key.

PRACTICAL PRACTICE
Hot Sauce Speed Up the Spell

Some folk practitioners swear by the use of spicy sauces and/or botanicals to speed up the time it takes for a spell to take effect. Add this magickal mixture to whatever spellwork you are doing that could use a boost of swiftness.

What You'll Need

Hot sauce

Red pepper (optional)

Black pepper (optional)

Jalapeño pepper or other spicy pepper (optional)

Small bowl

Utensil to stir ingredients

Air-tight container for storing the mixture (e.g., a resealable plastic bag)

What You'll Do

As with all spellwork, intention is the critical must-have component to ensure the efficacy of manifesting what you desire. Formulate your intention before combining your ingredients in a small bowl, then speak that intention confidently and assertively over the mixture as you fully incorporate the components using a spoon or other utensil. Use your dominant hand and stir clockwise, starting slowly and increasing your speed until you are whipping the ingredients together. Store the mixture for future use.

Possible Uses

Lessen the time it takes for a spell to take effect

Grocery Store Plants and Herbs

When it comes to food items, it is incredibly easy to find the things in the list that follows for use in many spells and correspondence lists. Knowing how to get these ingredients in the most effective and frugal way is essential in Thrifty Witchery. The grocery store is full of food-grade magickal products that can be used and adapted to not only fit your needs but also your budget. And you do not have to reserve these purchases for spells and rituals. You can go to the store for your lunch supplies and use a portion in your magick as well. If you are already buying apples, oranges, and bananas regularly, explore how these foods can also be used in spellcraft so that even if they rot, they will not also go to waste.

What follows is a list of several herbs and foods that are easily found in a grocery store and are often inexpensive and accessible for everyone. If the ingredients you purchase are fresh, you will need to dry them out before using them. The drying process used for herbs and plant life (covered in the foraging chapter) will work for any of the items on this list as well.

Always keep in mind that this list of botanicals and their corresponding magickal uses is only a guideline of common magickal uses. You are empowered to practice the magick that resides within you in the way that expresses your unique magickal DNA. What follows are suggestions, not rules. Think of them as a jumping-off point from which you can adapt as needed.

Healing

Blackberry has healing properties and can be used in protection and money magick.

Cinnamon corresponds to spirituality in general. It can be used in spells for success, healing, protection, love, luck, and prosperity. It is said to increase power, strength, psychic awareness, and passion.

Cucumber increases chastity, fertility, and healing.

Mint will help to protect and heal. It increases communication and vitality and can be used to attract the Divine.

Rosemary has healing properties. It can be used in spells involving love or lust and will help to improve memory, prevent nightmares, and purify.

Love

Apples can be used for works that involve love, friendship, healing, fertility, honoring the dead, and house blessing.

Avocado has magickal properties that align with love, lust, and beauty.

Basil corresponds to love, wealth, prosperity, and protection. It removes confusion, fear, and weakness. Basil can also be used to banish hostile spirits.

Chili pepper can be used in hex-breaking as well as magick related to fidelity and love.

Cloves work for banishing hostile or negative forces. They can raise spiritual vibrations and mental clarity. They are great for manifesting desires and work well in magick dealing with love, money, protection, purification, and kinship.

Figs are used in fertility spells and work well in love magick. They can also be used for divination.

Luck

Cabbage aligns with fertility spells but can also be used in magick that draws in a profit or good luck.

Corn can be used in divination. It will also work in protection magick and drawing in good luck.

Orange peel is amazing for luck and money magick. It can also be used in love spells.

Parsley calms and protects. It can be used in prosperity and luck magick.

Pineapple can be used to increase luck, money, and chastity.

Money

Allspice can be used to attract money, luck, and healing. It helps in obtaining desires, and it can add energy to any spell.

Cashews can be used in money magick.

Dill can be used in money magick. It is also known to protect, increase luck, and create lust.

Flax seed will ward off poverty. This is a great ingredient to add to money magick; it can also be used for healing and protection.

Nutmeg is helpful in money and prosperity magick. It will increase luck and protection. Additionally, this is a great spice to use in hex-breaking.

Protection

Anise seeds and seed pods (stars) are great for warding off the evil eye. They can help draw in happiness, enhance psychic abilities, and prevent bad dreams. Additionally, they can be used for purification and protection as well as to increase power and bring forth luck.

Bay leaf has properties that align with protection magick, good fortune, and success. It is great for purification, strengthening, healing, and increasing psychic awareness.

Black pepper is commonly used to banish negativity and protect against evil. It is said to increase courage as well.

Cayenne is a powerful ingredient for spells that repel negativity or create a separation. It can be used in purification magick and helps to speed up the magick of any mixture it is added to.

Chamomile is known for reducing stress, but it will also increase the success of a spell and help to remove hexes. Additionally, it works well in magick involving love, healing, meditation, sleep, and luck.

Garlic will help to heal, protect, and purify.

Purification

Coconut can be used for chastity, protection, and purification spells.

Grapefruit is excellent for purification.

Lime can purify and protect. It increases tranquility and strengthens love.

Marjoram can be used for purification and to rid yourself of negativity. It is also helpful in divination and protection.

Sage will purify, heal, and increase wisdom.

Sea Salt is used for cleansing, purification, grounding, and protection.

Wisdom

Almonds correspond with abundance, wisdom, money, prosperity, and healing.

Honey can be used to attract most anything.

Peaches are great for fertility spells and help draw in wisdom.

Sunflowers increase energy, power, and wisdom. They can be used for protection magick and manifesting goals.

One Person's Trash Is Another Person's Magick

Finding is not only the act of predetermining and locating something you want to use. It also works in reverse. You can view your environment and discover (or find) uses for things that may not seem like they have any more use left in them. In the purest form of reusing and recycling, a witch can take what is already in their house, or even more essentially, in their garbage, and give these found items new life. This is one of magick's true forms—not only are you enriching your practice and empowering yourself to use what you already have, you are also transmuting seemingly useless items into new tools and ingredients for your magick. This is a form of alchemy that literally transforms trash into magickal treasure.

As we mentioned earlier, many people own worn, broken, or out-of-date items that they have not quite disposed of yet. Instead of worrying about what does or does not fit into a tiny metaphysical box for your magickal use, take the time to evaluate new and creative ways to access your magick with items that are headed for the trash. Your house is full of products that may no longer be practically useful, but what if you could use them as part of your magickal practice? When you open your witch's eyes and look at these things in a new way you will find that there are useful applications for everything in the world of magick. You only need to find their purpose and then apply it.

Cosmetics

If you are a person who uses cosmetic products, you can repurpose expired liquid eyeliner to create and mark sigils and wards. As many people know, eyeliner is not the easiest of makeup products to remove. Using such an item on surfaces that are unlikely to ever interact with makeup remover only helps to increase the longevity of the markings you make with it.

Sidewalk Chalk

Old stubs of colored sidewalk chalk can be pulverized and then mixed with water to create a sort of paint. This can be used in all sorts of ways from marking out a circle to making sigils and wards. The resulting "paint" easily washes away, so permanence is not an issue, making it great for body work.

Broken Glass

The news has been full of amazing archaeological finds in the last few years. Sorcerer's kits full of beautiful stones and figures have been found in Pompeii and European countries[39] and an old witch jar was recently found in the space where a former confederate fort once stood.[40] From these findings we have learned that rusted nails were often placed in jars for protection from witchcraft, but broken glass in a spell jar can do the job just as well. It seems even our ancestors used some of what was destined for the trash pile and found new and meaningful purposes for it.

Old Clothes

Clothing that is too worn or stained to swap, pass down, or donate may have some surface areas that are perfectly fine; these can be snipped from the garment for fabrication as spirit bags or pouches for supplies such as divination cards, pentacles, or other altar pieces. One of the handiest qualities of fabric is that it can be manipulated to do all sorts of things. You can cut up old fabrics and create powerful magick with them,

....

39 Jason Daley, "A Sorceress' Kit Was Discovered in the Ashes of Pompeii" *Smithsonian* magazine online, August 14, 2019, https://www.smithsonianmag.com/smart-news/sorceresss-kit-was-discovered-ashes-pompeii-180972907/.

40 Chris Ciaccia, "Civil War-era 'Witch Bottle' Found in Virginia," Fox News, January 27, 2020, https://www.foxnews.com/science/civil-war-witch-bottle-found-virginia.

especially in the case of clothes. Our clothing is not just something we wear to cover our bodies; it is often an expression of who we are. As adults, many of us can choose our clothes. We actively decide what we want the world to see and know about us. The fabric becomes enmeshed with our personalities and our eccentricities. Using fabrics imbued with our own personal power enlivens and enhances the magickal workings that incorporate them.

Old Bed Linens

In the same way that our clothing holds our energy signature, so do our bed sheets. These are the swaddling that comforts us during the darkness of night. We lie on them feeling safe in our beds, and we trust that we will not only be protected while we sleep but also kept warm and covered. Threadbare sheets can have areas that are not worn through and can often be cut out into swatches of fabric large enough to use as an altar cloth. When we adorn our altars with items like this, we are not only incorporating a part of ourselves into our sacred space but are also blanketing the space with the same level of comfort and trust associated with their mundane function.

Old Board Games

Old board games or children's games that are missing pieces can also be repurposed for new and interesting uses in your magick. Look at them with a witch's eyes to see how they can be reused in witchy ways. Old playing boards can be refurbished to create all sorts of items from vision boards to a firm surface for tarot spreads to portable altars. You can do the same thing with folding cardboard playing surfaces, which can be covered over with images cut from magazines or pieces of saved wrapping paper. Just because you might be missing some of the letter tiles in a classic word-making game does not mean that the set needs to be tossed in the trash. You can save the tiles to spell out one-word intentions or keywords for the magick you are working on. Additionally, you could use them to create a divination practice much like casting lots. For example, you might pull a letter and then use just that letter to begin writing in a journal using alliteration or free-writing (anything that comes to mind) to receive messages from Spirit or Source. Or you could pull a series of letter tiles and see what words or phrases you can make, and then use that message as touchpoint for the rest of your day.

Broken Crayons

If you live with school-age children, they may bring home left-over classroom supplies at the end of the school year. Check for broken crayons. These seemingly useless sticks of wax have several uses in magickal practices. Most notably, they can be used to create candles. Also, crayon wax can be substituted for food coloring when making salt dough projects such as pentacles, sigils, or items representing each of the quarters for your altar. Melted crayons can also be poured into molds of various shapes. And if you develop or already have the talent for it, crayons can even be carved into representational shapes that could easily stand alone as altar pieces.

Old Jars

Old sauce jars or spice bottles can be cleaned, sanitized, and used to store apothecary items or materials such as bric-a-brac and beads for future use in witchy fabrications. Labels can be made from bits of paper taped or glued to the outside of the glass. If you want to dress up the labels a little, try burning the edges of your paper label to create interesting edges or perhaps draw one or two little stars or cauldrons on the labels. You do not have to be a professional artist or calligrapher to create a label that is a little funky and fun.

Reusing for Magick

Finding uses for what was once thought of as trash is not just a powerful way to develop and personalize your practice; it is also a wonderful way to honor the earth. Waste ends up in landfills that harm our planet too often. Typically, many witches are already aware of the effects we have on the land. To dive into your own trash and identify the ways in which you can use it instead of throwing it out is an effective way to grow closer to the planet and all the energies available for you to tap into.

PRACTICAL PRACTICE
Liquid Eyeliner Sigils

Both liquid and pencil eyeliners contain pigment in addition to agents that allow it to form a film and thicken. The thickeners can be made of waxes, gums, or clays. Eyeliners are made to stay on until cleaned off, which makes them great for applying sigils on washable surfaces. Cosmetics that are applied around the eye have a short shelf life due to bacteria concerns; generally, the best practice is to replace eyeliner every three to six months. But just because the product is no longer safe to use around your eyes does not mean that it cannot be effectively used for other purposes.

What You'll Need

    A few pieces of paper
    Writing implement
    Mirror (optional)
    Old eyeliner

What You'll Do

Sigils or symbols can be as streamlined or as elaborate as you desire. One way to create a sigil is to spell out your intention, distill it into one word, then use the letters of that word as the basis of your design. Another possible choice is to create a sigil from simple drawings that represent your intention (a heart for love, etc.), or you can do a combination of letters and symbols. Use your pieces of paper to refine your intention from a phrase into a word into a sigil that you feel accurately represents that intention. Access your wisdom and intuition while shaping the intention. If you are drawing the sigil on your body, decide where the most effective location will be to activate its energies. For example, if your intention is to speak the messages you receive from Source, placing sigils on your throat, near your lips, next to your ears, and/or over your heart will most effectively activate the energies of the sigil. Practice drawing the sigil a few times before marking with the eyeliner. State your intention aloud as you mark your sigil.

Possible Uses

    Ritual
    Protection
    Setting boundaries or wards

PRACTICAL PRACTICE
Ragbag Spirit Bag

You can fabricate all sorts of handy bags to use in your witch-craft. They can be large enough to hold a bone divination set, tarot or oracle decks, or small enough to hold crystals, pebbles, or feathers. Bags help keep your witchy supplies organized and, if you need to be discreet about your practice, can be effective ways to keep your tools hidden in plain sight. Another bonus to using outgrown or worn-out clothing to create your bags is that the material already carries some of the wearer's energy in it.

What You'll Need

> Old or frayed article of clothing
>
> Scissors
>
> Yarn, ribbon, or string long enough to tie bag closed
>
> Short bit of plastic straw (optional, for drawstring bags)

What You'll Do

Even old and tattered articles of clothing have sections that are still usable. Determine which witchy tool you'll be making the bag for; larger items require more material while smaller items need less. Cut a square of cloth from the cleanest, least frayed area of the fabric. Place your item(s) in the center of the square, draw the ends of the material up, and tie off with a length of yarn, ribbon, or string. If possible, be mindful of any color magick you might want to incorporate to complement the items you will keep in the bag.

Another method that is a little more involved yet still simple is to make a drawstring bag. Old short socks work well if you choose to go this route. Use a pair of scissors to snip two small holes on either end of the cuff at the top of a short sock. The drawstring can be anything from a shoelace to yarn to string, just make sure it will be long enough so that the ends can be tied to close the bag after you have threaded the drawstring through the cuff. It helps to have something small and stiff, like a bit of plastic straw, to thread one end of your drawstring into so that you can easily pull it through the cuff. Thread the drawstring through the cut on one end and pull it through to the other cut, then work the drawstring in the same way through the other side of the cuff to complete the loop. Adjust the drawstring so that there is an equal length on either end, tie the loose ends together.

Possible Uses

Any kind of pouch for supplies such as gemstones, bone divination sets, tarot or oracle decks, and luck or spirit bags.

PRACTICAL PRACTICE
Altar Cloth

While an altar cloth is not a must-have item, sometimes it is gratifying to change the look of your altar to correspond with the different seasons. Altar cloths can also transform bookshelves or other multi-use spaces or surfaces into an ambient setting more aligned with your rituals and spellcasting.

What You'll Need

> Old bedsheet (clean)
> Scissors
> Measuring device (a ruler or measuring tape)
> Sewing needle and thread (optional)
> Markers or paint to decorate (optional)

What You'll Do

Old solid-color sheets work well, but patterned sheets are also workable. Measure the surface you plan to make the altar cloth for. Determine if your old sheet has a large enough usable section to transform into a cloth, measure to cover altar area, and cut to size. If frayed edges are a concern, fold a small bit of the fabric along all sides of the cloth to form a finished edge and whipstitch into place using needle and thread. If desired, you can decorate your altar cloth using markers, paint, or used eyeliner.

Possible Uses

> Covering for altars or other surfaces when spellcasting or engaging in ritual.

Pennies on the Dollar

While you do not need to spend a single dime to juice and boost your spellcraft, there are times when you are actively attempting to find something but no free options exist. Does this mean that you are incapable of maintaining a penny-wise practice? Of course not—it simply means that occasionally you may need or want to buy an item that just cannot be found outside of a store. When this happens, try to be as thrifty as possible so that your budget is not blown sky high.

Here are some suggestions for getting the most return from your hard-earned cash.

End-of-Season Sales

In the United States, every approaching seasonal change brings about the same conversation for many people: "Can you believe they have Christmas (or Easter or Halloween or Thanksgiving) stuff out in the stores already?" Once called the "Christmas creep," this is a phenomenon that seems to start earlier every year, and not just for Christmas. It might not even be remotely near the end of the current season before the next batch of holiday-themed stuff crowds its way to the shelves. When the merchandise is in season, everything is pricey. Wouldn't it make more monetary sense to buy these things during the off-season when it is not so radically marked up?

From big box stores to retail giants and even your local small businesses and grocery stores, across the year retailers have end-of-season sales to clear the shelves for fresh inventory. It is all part of supply and demand—when demand is high, prices are high; when demand is low, prices are low. For example, it is common in January in the Northern Hemisphere to find bargains on fall and winter items. Spring and summer items generally go on clearance around July. During post-season sales, you can pick things up for up to 75 to 90 percent off of their original retail prices. You can gather what you may want to use as magickal tools, such as seasonally colored or themed candles, offering bowls, and décor in the off-season and save them for use when the season returns. You can use autumn- and winter-themed products such as pinecones, gourds, cornucopias, and more for altar pieces designated for your deities or ancestors. Spring and summer themed objects such as seashells,

Easter eggs, and shamrocks can be used in the same way. If you maintain a practice that focuses on the Wheel of the Year, you can use things purchased at the end of the winter season for future Litha, Mabon, Samhain, Yule, and Imbolc rituals. And anything purchased at the end of the summer season can be used to support your Ostara, Beltane, and Litha celebrations.

Even if you do not work with deities or ancestors, you can still use themed items to access the energy you may draw from a particular season. It is not uncommon for witches to feel an affinity for one season of year more than others. It is also common to feel drained during the time of year that is opposite from the season you align best with. Taking the time to set up a space that is infused with the essences of the season that best suits you, even when it is not during that season, can help to increase your energy and allow you to feel more comfortable in a less ideal time of year for you. Who says you can't decorate for Halloween or Samhain all year long? The same holds true for Christmas or Yule, Ostara, and Litha as well.

Another place to check for bargain prices on new items is online. Companies that feature surplus inventory often have steep discounts and, if you are okay with waiting a little while to get your purchases, are a great way to not only save but also to shop from home. Often you can search for the best prices on many different websites and then choose what fits best into your budget. This is an ideal way to maintain a thrifty approach to acquiring your magickal tools without breaking the bank.

Garage and Yard Sales

Church jumble/rummage sales and garage/yard sales can offer some terrific bargains. It may not seem like the most ideal place to find your witchy items, considering that many witches are recovering Christians, but church sales are a worthwhile place to discover items you can repurpose for use in your practice. Often there are gems in the rough in these sales, and while you may not find a cauldron or a new altar, it is not uncommon to find some bits and bobs that can be refurbished for your practice. Garage sales may feel a bit like foraging. What makes them an experience in finding is that you generally have some idea that you will find something of value somewhere in these purposefully collected goods, whereas in foraging you may or may not come across something you can use in your practice.

Estate sales—where frequently everything down to the studs in a house is for sale—can be the source of some truly spectacular finds. You will get more for your money if you wait until the last day, but if you come across an item that you believe is a must-have, you can still get a pretty good deal and can often haggle with whomever is running the sale down from the sticker price a little bit. Many times you can find old, broken jewelry that you can repurpose for your magickal practice or old board games whose parts you can repurpose for future spellwork.

Deep Discount Stores

Stores that offer steeply discounted prices can be a go-to shopping destination for the frugal witch. Shops in the United States such as Dollar Tree, the 99 Cent Store, Family Dollar, and others carry seasonal items that you can incorporate into your witchy lifestyle, while wholesalers such as Costco and Sam's Club can also save you some serious money. An additional bonus to purchasing in bulk at a wholesaler is that you can barter or trade within your community whatever you did not use from your purchase for other things you can. You can be even gentler on your budget by keeping an eye out for clearance sales at big box stores.

Thrift stores can offer bargains if you're a canny buyer. For example, many thrift stores are busiest over the end of the weekend, usually with shoppers and homeowners dropping off items that did not sell at garage sales. This means that for the first couple of days of the week, there will be fresh inventory on the racks and shelves. Just like with retail stores, deep discount stores are somewhat seasonal—they will often have fresher inventory after people have done some spring or winter cleaning in their closets.

Going-Out-of-Business Sales

This is exactly what it sounds like: sometimes despite their best efforts, stores and businesses go out of business and will try to clear as much inventory as they can before they must shut down permanently. Waiting until the very end of the going-out-of-business sale can garner discounts of up to 75 to 90 percent. Just remember not to get carried away by the steep discounts—the goal is to spend as thriftily as possible.

Cleaning and Cleansing Your Found Items

Cleaning and cleansing your found items before putting them to magickal use will help ensure that they are fully prepared to be loaded with your intentions. Found fabrics should be cleaned as recommended by the manufacturer; items such as used crayons should be free of paper sleeves, and glass jars should be cleaned with soap and water and then sterilized by immersing them into boiling water for about five minutes.

Wooden items can be cleaned with a damp cloth, most stones and crystals can be cleaned with some soapy water, and many ceramic items can be cleaned with cleaning vinegar, which is slightly more acidic than white vinegar and can be purchased at the grocery store. Cleaning vinegar can be diluted with liquid soap and water; you'll still want to wear some plastic or rubber gloves, as cleaning vinegar can irritate your hands and fingernails. Slightly tarnished silver items can be cleaned using simple dish soap, warm water, soft cloths, and lots of elbow grease. After rubbing the soap mixture into the silver item with a soft cloth, run cold water over it and buff with a second dry, soft cloth. You can also use a cornstarch paste to clean tarnished silver. Use two parts water to one part cornstarch, blend, apply the paste to the item, and allow to dry for about fifteen minutes. Wash off with a damp cloth and buff with a dry cloth.

After you have thoroughly cleaned your found items, cleanse them of any metaphysical energies that may still be lingering. Often you have no way of knowing the history of any items you have decided to bring into your practice, so it is wise to spend a little time cleansing your future tools in addition to the practical cleaning you've done. One of the simplest and most effective ways to cleanse items is either with a daylong sun bath or nightlong moon bath. Use common sense when deciding how you want to cleanse your items; for example, crayons may soften and melt after spending the day under the sun's cleansing rays, so a moon bath would be a better choice to promote cleansing. Salt is another cleansing option that you will want to exercise some discernment in using. Items that would be corroded by direct contact with salt can instead be placed within a protective circle of salt for twenty-four hours. Whichever cleansing method you choose, chanting, singing, or saying a short charm while you put your cleanse into place will help boost the process.

Practical Practice
Salt Water for Cleansing

Water has been used for spiritual cleansing since the time of the ancient Greeks, and cultures all over the world consider water to be an integral part of their spiritual practices. Because water is almost everywhere and is, for many people, very accessible, we may tend to take its profound power for granted. This simple magickal working not only provides you with an all-purpose cleanser but also offers you an opportunity to strengthen your relationship with water energies.

What You'll Need
> Water (fresh, ocean, or rain if possible, but charged tap
> water works equally well)
> Salt (if you are not using sea water)
> Container (glass if possible)

What You'll Do
Tap Water: First, give thanks for the gift of water. Add a few grains of salt to the tap water and put the filled container out all night (moon water) or all day (sun water). As you set your container of salted water out, think about the characteristics

of the energies the liquid will be absorbing and how those energies will be used to support the integrity of the cleansing you plan to perform. Choose a focus word, gaze at your container of salted water, and push that intention into it. Retrieve your salted water the next morning (moon water) or evening (sun water) and use according to your intention.

Other Waters: Fresh, ocean, and storm waters already have a lot of energetic dynamism specific to their place of origin. Stream and river waters carry one type of energy, while lakes embody another. Oceanic waters have strong primal energies, as do storm waters. Give thanks for the water and, if the water you have collected is not oceanic, add a few grains of salt to it and think about how you plan to use this water. Select a focus word and push that intention into the water, then use according to your intention.

Possible Uses

Casting circles

Drawing sigils on doors, walls, and yourself

Cleansing large areas (flicking)

Consecrating items

Frugality and Finding

Finding is the most structured aspect of Thrifty Witchery. You set your intention and then go out and look until that intention is manifest. Whether you locate something you need in a pile of things you meant to throw away or repurpose a trinket for use on the tip of a wand you may craft, finding allows you both the freedom and insight to see the world differently.

Choosing the herbs, oils, or spices for your witch-crafting based on what you already have engages your witchy creativity and helps to get you thinking outside of the box. The same can be said about looking through the trash or recycling bins to find containers for your spells. Just because something seems like trash does not mean that you cannot find a good, practical, magickal use for it. Taking the time to evaluate what you already own and deciding if you can find a use for any of it is truly a magickal act in its own regard.

Finally, knowing where to seek the things you want or need in your practice and being able to afford them without blowing your existing budget is incredibly empowering. It is proof that you are a strong, powerful, and sovereign witch. Learning to sharpen your finding skills will lead you to a greater understanding of just how deeply within you your magick runs.

CHAPTER 8
Fabricating

Fabricating is the third of the tangible components of Thrifty Witchery. Intuition, wisdom, and intention are an esoteric combination of magickal access. These three modalities are present in foraging and finding, but it is in fabricating that they come together and give birth to practical physical objects. Fabrication is the aggregate of not only foraging and finding and intuition, wisdom, and intention, but is also concrete evidence of your self-empowerment and the magick that exists within you.

In foraging is an understanding that the world around you is your magickal warehouse. You begin to intentionally experience your environment and how it responds to intuition and wisdom. In finding, you access the ability to see and make connections between the various objects that have called to you. You gain insight into how to determine what you specifically need before going to the location where you are most likely to obtain it. Additionally, with finding you begin to assign new uses for what you once thought was useless, thus finding new purpose for what would have otherwise been discarded. This engages aspects of both intention and wisdom.

It is through the fabrication of your magickal tools and items that you finally gather all you have learned and gained access to in your self-empowered spellcraft. You mix those elements together to garner tangible results. No longer are the philosophies of intuition, wisdom, and intention simply abstractions. They become manifest in the act of fabricating.

What Is Fabricating?

Fabricating is an act of alchemy, the transformation of separate components into an admixture that becomes something new, something more than the sum of its parts. In it, you literally manifest your desired outcome into the physical world and imbue that manifestation with your energies. Your act becomes one of not only manufacturing an item but imparting a piece of yourself into what you produce. When you fabricate your tools, your magickal items become a part of you in an intimate way that cannot be replicated in anything you could ever purchase in a store.

Fabricating your tools represents, on a microscopic level, the change you are seeking to manifest on the macroscopic level. In other words, through the personal act of creating items you want to own, you are effectively designing the tools you deem necessary to affect real change in both your magick-making and your environment. In doing so you set into motion a sequence of actions that begin as a small spark and ignite powerful ripples that flow into every action you take, magickal and mundane.

Your tools themselves are energetic bridges—connectors that transport your will toward your purpose. You infuse your created tools with your magick and make a statement that you are, in a sense, attempting to gain control of your outcomes. Crafting something in the physical world is making the conscious decision to act intentionally. Knowing that, your actionable response to any situation is both valid and powerful. For example, say you have crafted a necklace for the sole purpose of protection. Not only is there protective magick infused into this necklace, there is also a sense of self-empowerment in wearing your creation because you have literally birthed your magick into being. You created something and loaded it with your intuition, wisdom, and intention. When you wear it daily it becomes a physical reminder of the very real effort you put into the defenses you have built. Focus objects like this springboard your desire out into the universe. They say, "Hey, this action is valid, this behavior is effective, and the work I have put into my magick is always active."

As we mentioned earlier, the fabricated item represents the culmination of what you have gathered through your foraging and finding. It is often the endgame in developing your magickal toolkit. You have used your wisdom to identify how to use an object. You have used your intuition to help you find the pieces that will ultimately comprise the resulting tool. Your intentions for what the item's purposes have been set.

Much like intention, fabricating has a bilateral role. It is dynamic in that in one sense, fabricating simply is the physical act of making an object. You decided what to make and then made it. But, in the same way that intention serves as a bridge connecting your metaphysical will to your expressed will, when fabricating a piece for your magickal purposes you are also bridging your metaphysical intentions into physical ones. You essentially are manifesting the totality of your self-empowerment, intuition, wisdom, and intention into magickal action.

The tangible object you fabricated is also a conveyor, a focus item that accumulates and directs your metaphysical will. You did not just casually create something cute—you gathered your intentions, wisdom, and intuition and forged something through magickal processes into an item that now holds a magick intrinsically yours. You took the time to forage for the pieces that called to you. You actively pursued the items that you needed to find. And then you combined that with all the magick you possess and coalesced it into a single article of your own design.

In truth, when a witch is fabricating anything, they are essentially taking a piece of themselves and placing it into the item. These charged tools allow you to tap into a much deeper part of yourself, giving you the power boost needed to see your desired intentions come to fruition. Through fabrication, your self-empowerment becomes synergistic and ever flowing.

PRACTICAL PRACTICE
Simple Salt-Dough Tools

You can make a remarkable number of witchy tools using a simple salt dough. The fact that salt dough is made of three ingredients—flour, water, and salt—just adds to the magick. You can boost that inherent magick even further by incorporating all the elements into your creations. Earth and water are already present in the dough; add the element of air by breathing your intentions onto the salt-dough objects just before you add the element of fire (baking in an oven).

What You'll Need

Medium to large bowl

Flat surface to work on, such as a table or counter

Plain white flour

Plain table salt

Water

Wooden spoon

Wax paper or cling wrap (optional)

Something to roll dough flat, such as a rolling pin or
heavy dowel

Knife to cut shapes and inscribe sigils

What You'll Do

Place the bowl on your work surface. Add flour and salt using
a ratio of 4 cups flour to 1 cup table salt. Slowly add in 1½
cups water. Stir the mixture using a wooden spoon. When the
dough becomes too difficult to stir, turn it out onto the work
surface. If possible, use cling wrap, parchment paper, or wax
paper both under and over the dough to keep it from sticking
to the counter and the rolling pin. Otherwise, be sure to heav-
ily flour both the work surface and the rolling pin to reduce
the dough's stickiness. Knead the dough by hand a few minutes until pliable—it should feel like modeling clay. Next, roll
the dough out to about ⅛" thick.

Begin to shape and inscribe your tools from the dough. You
can make things like long snake-like rolls and fashion them
into flat spirals reminiscent of a labyrinth. Pentacles, keys, tri-
quetras, snakes, and even runes can be made from salt dough.
Mark designs on the dough before baking and, if you plan to
hang your creation as a decoration, be sure to make a little hole
in the dough for the ribbon or string. After shaping and inscribing your tools, bake in a low oven (300 °F / 148 °C) for 1 hour
or until hard. After baking and when the creation has cooled
completely, you can embellish using simple paints, markers, or
whatever you have on hand.

Possible Uses

    Runes for divination

    Pentacles for altars or decoration

    Representations of sacred items / symbols to your deity(ies), ornaments for Yule trees

What Happens When You Fabricate?

Creating your own witchy tools from scratch—that is, from essentially nothing—gives you the opportunity to literally manifest exactly the items that you identify as worth owning for your practice with your own two hands. This is how magick works in its most basic terms. You set your intentions for what you want and then set out to obtain it through not just your actions but also your intuition, wisdom, and intention. When you look at all of what you have collected, you could regard the bits of string, broken jewelry, sticks, dirt, crayons, rocks, shells, bones, and the rest of society's castoffs as other people's junk, but when you look again with a witch's eyes and mind, you begin to see that junk in terms of possibilities and potentials. As stated in the last chapter, what might seem to be trash can hold so much potential when you choose to see the possibility of what it can become.

Fabricating is the innovative heart of Thrifty Witchery, and many folk magicians and witches use this pennywise approach to crafting their tools. Accessing what the land has to offer, finding purpose for the seemingly useless, and merging the two together into new and useful items is a kind of reclaiming. It is in this action that a witch asserts their power, their magick.

How would your sense of self-empowerment change if you chose to view crafting your own tools not as a last resort because you do not have money to buy what you need or want, but instead as the *first* choice because you believe to your core that in creating your own tools you are living your witchery in the most fundamental and authentic way possible?

When you take ownership of your craft, when you create, your empowerment is self-evident. You did not need to go to a store to purchase candles because you made your own from broken crayons and the leftover wax sitting at the bottom of a store-bought candle. You figured out how to make a wick that works from a broken shoestring. You decided to infuse your own ingenuity with a desire to cast magick that brings your intention to life.

Fabrication is, in essence, your drive to get the magickal job done. It validates and grounds you in your self-empowerment. It engages your creativity and opens a channel to access your intuition, inviting your innate perceptions to embody themselves in your creations. It is, in effect, conjuration.

In the previous chapter on finding, we mentioned endorphins, those "feel-good" hormones that your central nervous system releases when you activate your internal reward system. The same thing happens in fabrication. In her article, "Endorphins: Effects and how to increase levels" author Jennifer Berry writes:

> Natural endorphins work similarly to opioid pain relievers, but their results may not be as dramatic. However, endorphins can produce a "high" that is both healthy and safe, without the risk of addiction and overdose.[41]

....

41 Jennifer Berry, "Endorphins: Effects and how to increase levels," Medical News Today website, February 6, 2018, https://www.medicalnewstoday.com /articles/320839.

You may have experienced this effect after successfully casting a spell or participating in a particularly powerful ritual. When you make your own tools and witchy accoutrements, you can experience the same rush of endorphins as well as a deep sense of personal satisfaction. You should be proud of what you have fabricated, and not just because it is your creation, birthed from a coalition of your mind, your hands, and Spirit-driven actions. You should be proud of your creations because they are your little witch tool babies, brought into the world and designed to work for you.

However, we do not want to give you the impression that fabricating your own supplies is all fluffy bunnies and soft kitties. When creating anything, there is likely to be some form of sweat, tears, and sometimes even blood.

Consider for a moment the power that resides within your bodily fluids. Our DNA is in our spit; maybe you used it to wet the thread when you pushed it through the eye of a needle to sew whatever it is you are making. Saliva is also often used to trace ancestral DNA, to tell us where we come from, who we descend from. And when placed under a microscope and analyzed, our blood can tell us most of what is happening inside our bodies. If you accidentally slice yourself with a blade using to cut some material, it is likely some of that blood will be added to what you are making. Sometimes while fabricating our tools, we incorporate parts of our physical self, such as hair or fingernail clippings, into our items as well. It is not just energy and intention that we combine into our fabrications.

There is some physical labor involved—remember, magick always exacts a cost—and there will certainly be times when you think about how much easier it would be to just buy the stuff you need. And you would be right; it would be easier. If your frustration with the process of manufacturing your own tools bubbles over, sometimes buying might be the way to dial down the tension. But ask yourself this: would that be as fulfilling?

If you find yourself frustrated with fabricating your witchy tools, ask yourself how your perspective of the more difficult aspects of fabricating might change if you approached them as a meditative practice.

A Practice of Mindfulness

As an example, let's explore mindfulness while fabricating twig pentacles. Twigs can be a little fiddly to work with; they do not stay exactly in place as you bind them together, and they may twist and roll as you work to set and fix them into position. The binding materials may also be fiendishly uncooperative. Your fingers may feel particularly clumsy, you may feel your muscles tensing or notice that your neck is becoming uncomfortably stiff. Particularly if you have perfectionist tendencies, fashioning twig pentacles can devolve into exercises in frustration, negative self-talk, and defeatism.

When we approach this task as a mindfulness meditation, our perspective is not the only thing that changes. The energies we bring to the task change as well. We no longer bathe the twigs and bindings in auras of resentment, impatience, and frustration. Instead, we imbue them with a sense of rightness, contentment, and peace by way of our brain's alpha waves, which are produced when the brain is in a relaxed, wakeful state.

Mindfulness meditation specifically is a process of being fully in the moment, completely inhabiting whatever action (or non-action) the body is performing. Let's look at how this might work when fabricating a twig pentacle.

Begin by laying out the materials listed below onto a clean, clutter-free workspace. If possible, reduce as many distractions as you can—if the television is on, turn it off. If you are multi-tasking, wait until you can give your full attention to crafting your twig pentacle. While many people find silence conducive to meditation, just as many people experience silence as another type of distraction. If mood music is something that works well for you, play it softly while you prepare your materials and yourself for a magickal interaction.

Sit or stand in front of the materials you have arranged on your workspace. Allow your eyelids to relax. Slowly draw in a deep bellyful of oxygen through your nostrils, holding the air in your belly for a few seconds before releasing the carbon dioxide your body naturally produces through your gently pursed lips. Do this at least three times while releasing any tension your muscles may be holding.

As you are breathing, think about the symbiotic relationship with the planet that your inhales and exhales represent. The carbon dioxide you exhale supports the plant life on our earth, including the tree that produced your twigs. The trees release oxygen as a by-product when they make use of the carbon dioxide we exhale. Visualize this interconnectedness as you continue to breathe.

Rest your hands, palms open and up, on the workspace or on your thighs while you are breathing. Become aware of the heat emanating from your palms. Direct your intention to imbue your twig pentacle with magickal power toward your palms and give yourself a few moments to allow that intention to coalesce in your hands.

Open your eyes fully. Draw one final bellyful of breath through your nostrils, hold it a few seconds, then slowly release that breath through pursed lips directly onto your materials, holding in mind your magickal intention.

Before assembling your pentacle, touch, hold, and/or stroke each twig and speak a gratitude upon it.

This mindfulness meditation is not something you "have to" or "ought to" do every single time you want to create twig pentacles, but it is worth trying every now and then simply to further ground yourself in your identity as a witch. Remember, magick is not just something you do—it is in your DNA. It is what you are whether awake, asleep, during the day, at night, and everything in between.

PRACTICAL PRACTICE
Twig Pentacle

We witches love our pentacles! These five-pointed stars have been around since ancient Greek and Babylonian times and, particularly if you are still in the broom closet, are an easy way to express your witchiness while hiding in plain sight.

What You'll Need

    Five straight sticks, all approximately the same length
    Twine, ribbon, string, or some other material used for
      tying
    Scissors

What You'll Do

On a flat work surface, lay out your sticks in the shape of a star, making sure the ends overlap. Adjust the sticks as needed for the best fit. Using your binding material, wrap any point where two sticks intersect on the outside of the star and tie off; cut off excess binding from the outside of the knot. Continue this process on every star tip, then repeat the process where branches cross in the interior of the star. Every place where two sticks cross should be bound.

Possible Uses

> Decorating wand tips
> Yule tree decorations
> Altar decoration

A Practice of Patience

Homemade oil infusions can require a lot of time, attention, and work to create. While satisfying, the fabrication process can be frustrating and tiresome. It is in these moments that you might ask yourself what is causing the tension. Whose rubric are you basing your progress on? You are fabricating what you need, and these items are not for anyone else. Even if something you are creating is outside of your skill set, you can still continue. Fabricating is a practice—as such, you will find that over time, you will become better at making the tools you want.

PRACTICAL PRACTICE
Infused Oils

Oils can be used for all sorts of things from a base for daily-use potions to creating infusions for dressing candles. Infused oils are much milder (though no less potent) than essential oils and can be used on your skin without irritation. Creating an oil that you can anoint yourself with is helpful for grounding, protection, and several other purposes. Brewing up batches of oils infused with the ingredients for a particular need is an excellent way to put in the work ahead of time so that your routine magickal maintenance can be accomplished the moment you need it. Once an oil is brewed for whatever use you have intended, you can then apply it daily as you would a perfume—it is magick on the go! Oils can be infused using either a cold or a hot method.

One important caveat to creating and using oils for magickal purposes is awareness of which herbs and ingredients are poisonous but commonly used in magick; never infuse these herbs into an oil that you plan to wear. Should you decide to use poisonous ingredients, *only* infuse them using a container that will never be used to cook, eat or drink out of, or contain foods intended for consumption. Poisonous herbs and ingredients pose a high risk of danger, up to and including death. Please be responsible and cautious when creating infusions with poisonous ingredients.

What You'll Need: Cold Infusion

> Dried herbs selected to support the specific purpose of your spell
>
> Oil, such as olive or another skin-friendly oil
>
> A mason jar and lid
>
> Coffee filter or cheesecloth
>
> A sunny place to set the filled mason jar in

What You'll Do: Cold Infusion

If they are not already dried or powdered, this should be the first thing you do with your herbs. If you have foraged them, you will want to rinse them off and dry them thoroughly. Water can cause your oil to become rancid and cloudy. Fresh herbs have a high water content, so drying them out on a lined sheet pan in a low oven is always an excellent way to ensure that your oil is long-lasting and usable. This process is detailed in the foraging chapter.

After cleaning and drying your jar thoroughly, fill it about three-quarters full with your herbs. Next, fill the jar right up to the brim with your oil. All the herbs should be fully submerged.

The oil will take about two months to fully infuse. Write down the date that you start your oil. Eight weeks can be difficult to track mentally, so having the start date in writing is helpful. Place your jar in a window that gets plenty of sunlight and moonlight. This supports the creation of your oil in both practical and magickal ways. The sunlight will not only heat the oil (helping the infusion process) but will also charge the oil with sun energy. The moon will go through almost two full cycles while your oil is infusing. This will allow you to draw down whatever aspect of the moon's power works best for your intention while also imbuing the oil with a well-rounded spectrum of moon energy. Each day, take some time to gently shake the oil jar and speak your intention into the oil to infuse it with your specific purpose.

When the eight weeks have passed, use a coffee filter or cheesecloth to strain the oil from the infusion jar into a new container, separating the herbs from the oil. Cap and store the oil in a cool, dark space such as your pantry. Discard the used herbs.

What You'll Need: Hot Infusion
> Herbs selected to support the specific purpose of your spell
> Oil, such as olive, coconut, or another skin-friendly oil
> Mason jar and lid
> Saucepan, slow cooker, or double boiler

What You'll Do: Hot Infusion
There are two methods for fabricating hot infusion oil. Chose whichever works best for you.

Mason Jar and Saucepan Method
Place your herbs in the container you will use to heat them up in. If you are using the Mason jar and saucepan method, you will place the herbs in the jar filling it about halfway full and then fill almost to the brim with your oil. Do not fill to the top because you will need space to stir the oil. It is best to use a saucepan not used to cook food, as some of your oil and herbs may remain in the saucepan. Some herbs you are using may not be food grade, and some may even be poisonous. It is always best to use reasonable caution when working with poisonous plants as they may leave a residue. Fill the saucepan with water

so that the water comes about halfway up the Mason jar. Be sure to monitor the water level in the saucepan so it never boils away, which would destroy your saucepan, burn the herbs and oil, and possibly break the Mason jar.

Crockpot and Double Boiler Methods

If you are using a crockpot or a double boiler, be sure that you do not use either of these items for any other purpose than making heat-infused oils.

In the crockpot method, place your herbs on the bottom and then pour in your oil until the herbs are fully submerged. Set the temperature on its lowest setting. You will need to monitor your concoction because if it gets too hot, your oil and herbs will simply burn and you will need to start over or use a different method. Do a test run with your crockpot prior to using any herbs and oil to see if this method will work with your equipment.

In the double boiler method, cover the herbs with oil in the top half of your double boiler. Add water to the bottom half of your double boiler. Again, you will need to monitor your concoction to make sure the water does not completely evaporate, lest the oil and herbs to burn and ruin the bottom half of your double boiler.

Place the double boiler on the stove or other heat source and bring to a slow simmer, not a hard boil. Allow the oil and herbs to remain on the heat for 12 hours while you are awake and able to check on it.

For all three methods, be sure to spend time stirring in a clockwise or counterclockwise motion using your dominant or nondominant hand depending on your intention. If you are drawing something in with your magick, stir clockwise using your dominant hand while repeating your intention. If you are sending something away, stir in a counterclockwise motion using your nondominant hand while repeating your intention. You do not need to stir the oil the entire 12 hours, but you should be sure to give the brew regular attention throughout the decoction process.

Once completed, allow your oil to cool completely. Then use a cheesecloth or coffee filter to strain the herbs from the oil as you pour it in its storage jar. Discard the herbs, and cap and store the oil in a cool, dark place such as your pantry.

Possible Uses
> Protection
> Grounding
> Warding
> Boosting specific energies

Fabricating Is a Gift to the Planet

Where there is a witch, there is a way, and indeed there are many ways to witch that do not resemble anything you might recognize as witchcraft. Whatever path a witch walks is valid—some practices are deity-based while others are atheistic; some are more esoteric while others have a more practical approach; some are lineaged while others are eclectic. There are practices that are all of these, some of these, and none of these; the variations are endless. As multi-corded as spellcrafting and witchery may be, one thing that the many strands of witchcraft might agree on is that a vast number of witches hold a deep respect and reverence for the earth.

We use parts of the earth in both mundane and magickal ways. We are dependent on the planet's resources that, while vast, are not unlimited. Yet there are wasteful practices that destroy our globe on a regular basis. Many of us in the witchcraft community tend to be aware of the damage humans do and take actions to mitigate it, and fabrication of our tools is one action we can take. The basic idea is this: when you fabricate your own tools, you are saving some of your hard-earned cash. On a more nuanced level, when you make the conscious choice to create your own tools as a tangible expression of your respect and reverence for the earth, you are saving your planet. You do not need to be a Green Witch or an Earth Witch to maintain a mindset of protecting or saving the planet. In fact, the idea that fabricating your own products helps save the earth could be a complete afterthought or coincidence to you. Even so, that is what is happening when you choose to fabricate. When you create your own tools, you cut the emissions created from the delivery of products. Fabricating anything yourself reduces the energy expended by factories mass-producing items to fill shelves worldwide. Choosing to reuse, refurbish, and repurpose what you already have cuts down on the waste that comprises landfills.

You may have heard the phrase "think globally, act locally," attributed to Scottish sociologist and conservationist Patrick Geddes (1854–1932). Essentially, it means that small actions can produce significant change that, as it happens, nicely aligns with the philosophies undergirding spellcraft. Of course, not everything you will refurbish or repurpose to fabricate your tools will be organic, but you will be at least keeping the inorganic materials out of the local landfill for a few more years. And though it may not feel like much of a difference to the health of our planet, multiply a practice of Thrifty Witchery across the world or even just one continent and you can see how much of an impact everyone acting locally could have globally.

PRACTICAL PRACTICE
Broken Glass Hex

In sixteenth- and seventeenth-century Great Britain, witch bottles were a common way to deflect negative magickal workings that may have been cast on a person. These objects contained things such as bent nails, urine, strands of hair, nail clippings, and broken glass, and were then buried in the ground. The intention was to cause whoever had cast the original offensive spell great pain, in effect boomeranging the negativity back to them. Additionally, the belief was that as soon as the person stopped hexing the target, their own pain would also stop.

What You'll Need

A bottle or jar with a lid
Bent nails or pins
Poppet representing the person you are reverse-hexing
Broken glass or mirror
Urine
Black candle to seal jar (optional)
Place to bury the jar
Shovel or hand spade

What You'll Do

As with all spellwork, be very detailed, specific, and thorough when crafting your intention. You do not want any backsplash or for the spell to affect anyone except its intended recipient.

As you create your poppet, keep your intention in mind and be crystal clear that this hex is directed solely in their direction. Your poppet does not need to be fancy; it can be as simple as a paper doll with the person's name written on it. Place the poppet in the jar and add the rest of the ingredients while stating your intention with conviction and with all your energies aligned toward that intention. The ingredients do not need to fill the jar to the brim. Seal the jar and, if desired, drip wax from a lit black candle around the edges of the lid to form an extra seal.

Bury the bottle upside down either in an outdoor area that will be relatively undisturbed or in the dirt of a large potted indoor plant.

Possible Uses

    Protection

    Hex-reversal

    Hexing

It's About Time

By now, you may be thinking to yourself, "I haven't got time to do what I have to do already, let alone trying to find time to fabricate all of my tools!" *Wall Street Journal* writer Laura Vanderkam offers this insight: "Instead of saying 'I don't have time' try saying 'it's not a priority,' and see how that feels."[42]

....

42 Adam Dachis, "Instead of Saying 'I Don't Have Time' Say 'It's Not a Priority,'" Lifehacker website, March 13, 2012, https://lifehacker.com/instead-of-saying-i-dont-have-time-say-its-not-a-pr-5892948.

You might find this an effective way to reevaluate how your time is spent. There is no question that some of the things soaking up your time are non-negotiable: employment, transportation, appointments, and activities related to daily living such as getting and preparing food, keeping your living space tidy, laundry, and more demand chunks of your time. Add into that any caregiving, parenting, or relationship activities, and there goes more time. It's time well spent, to be sure, but these obligations still translate to less time for activities in support of your witchcrafting. However, there may be ways to eke out a few scraps of time here and there. For instance, many of the fabrication projects we have mentioned can be done as a family or with children.

The idea is not to cram every available waking moment with some sort of activity. Everyone—even witches—needs downtime free of thinking about or doing anything. Often as not, downtime can mean plopping down in front of the television for an evening of channel surfing that leaves us wondering where the time went at the end of the evening.

If you want to bring your identity as a witch a little more center stage, you may want to try mindfully apportioning time spent in front of the television. Try to resist passing any kind of judgment on yourself. You are not creating a new way to self-shame; you are collecting data. Keep a brief log of your television-watching for two weeks or so, long enough to get a feel for how much time overall you might have available on a particular evening. You do not need to keep track of *what* you are watching, just the amount of time spent.

Next, make a list of the television shows that you really like, not the ones that just happen to be on as you are vegging in front of the screen but ones you are really invested in. Note the length of each show. Try to keep your favorites list short, no more than three if possible. Deduct the total of that time from the total amount of time measured in your logbook.

What are the results of your observations? Are there any blocks of time you may not previously have been aware of? You may find that you have more workable bits of discretionary time on some nights more than others, or that some of the chunks of your downtime really are not big enough for any kind of fabricating project. And let's face it: there may be some evenings when you are completely out of gas with no mental, spiritual, or physical energy left to spend on fabricating, no matter how it fuels your self-empowerment and witchery. That is completely okay. The point of this exercise is to offer you some simple tools to help you discover some small pockets of time to do your witchcrafting, not to make you feel like you are not doing enough.

Many of us have busy lives, and it is vastly helpful to completely stop, shut down your brain, and watch a show or even binge-watch a whole series. There are the projects that could be done while you have shut your brain down. Fabricating does not need to always demand complete focus. When it is convenient, multitasking is fine. You can sit on the couch watching the latest reality show while braiding string for a new necklace. It is okay to roll through a spooky movie marathon while sewing sachets out of old clothing. All of these are forms of active rest, and what it looks like for your life is entirely up to you.

Audiobooks are another great way to help make active resting work in your favor. Many of the more popular witchcraft and magick books are in audio format. If you find yourself wanting to work on a project and also read a book, why not do both? This format has become popular as our lives have become so busy. We listen to books while commuting to work or at our workstations, so why not listen while you craft as well? How much more immersed in your witchery might you feel when learning new and interesting witchcraft while also crafting your own tools?

PRACTICAL PRACTICE
Crayon Candles and Carvings

Many times, you may want to add a little color boost to support the magick you are working on. Green for money or fertility spells, red or pink for passion or love, yellow for abundance, or candles with colors corresponding to the different quarters— there are plenty of opportunities to use some colored candle energies in your witchcraft. You can DIY these easily using the wax from melted tea lights combined with melted broken crayon pieces.

What You'll Need
> Undyed cotton twine
>
> Scissors
>
> Surface for wicks to dry on, such as a paper towel or wax paper
>
> Water
>
> Small pan to boil water
>
> Wax from tea lights
>
> Clean, dry glass jars; 1 jar to melt tea light wax in for dipping your twine wicks, 1 set of jars to melt crayons and

wax in, another set of jars to pour your completed candle mixture in (used baby jars or jelly jars work well)

Toothpicks or skewers

Broken crayon pieces, separated by color

Something to hold the twine in place as the wax hardens,
such as a clothespin

What You'll Do

To prepare the wicks: Cut the cotton twine to make the wicks.
Measure how much twine you will need by measuring how
much wax you plan to pour into the container and adding 2
to 3 inches to the twine length so that the wicks will be able
to emerge from the top of the hardened wax. The wicks are
going to be dipped into the melted wax, so be sure you have a
surface for them to dry on, such as a paper towel.

Set a few inches of water to boil in the pan over medium
heat; the water should come a few inches up the sides of the
jar you will be melting your wax in. Remove the tea lights
from their casings and add several to a jar, then place the jar
into the pan of simmering water. As wax melts, remove the
small wicks from the tea lights. Add twines to the melted wax,
using a toothpick or skewer to fully immerse and coat them.
Remove coated twines from the melted wax and set them
aside on a paper towel to dry. Make sure they're straight.

To prepare the candle ingredients: Remove any paper that
might still be attached to the crayons. Remove some tea lights
from their containers. Using a ratio of 2 parts wax to 1 part
crayon, put the crayon bits and the tea lights into a fresh jar
(not the same one you dipped your twine into) and place
the jar into the pan of simmering water. Use a toothpick

or skewer to stir the components together as they melt and remove the small wicks from the tea lights.

To assemble the candle: Dip the end of one of the wicks into the melted crayon and tea light wax mixture. Center and set that end in the bottom of the jar you will be using to make your candle; hold the wick in place using something (a clothespin works fine) resting at a right angle over a toothpick that has been placed over the rim of the jar. Gently pour melted crayon and tea light mixture into the jar and allow it to fully harden, at least an hour and possibly longer depending on the amount of material you are using. Trim wick to about ¼" above the hardened candle before using.

Possible Uses

> Seasonal decor
> Quarter candles for altar
> Candle scrying

The Enemy of Good

When you choose to fabricate your witchy supplies, you are also making a choice to do some shadow work. Shadow work involves shining a light, exploring, and resolving all the negative messages that might bubble up from the cauldron of your psyche, those thoughts that say you are not good enough, you are not achieving enough, or in this case, every witchy tool you make looks like crap.

Perhaps you have heard a variation of the aphorism "perfect is the enemy of good." Particularly in Western culture, we are saturated with near-constant subliminal messaging and conditioning to always be striving for perfection and never settling for anything less. We are taught to never be satisfied, to always be thirsting for something more or better. When you start to fabricate your own witchy things, you are almost certainly going to run into some negative self-messaging. The question is not how to avoid this particular shadow; the question is how to deal with these feelings and bring them under control so that you can take pride in what you fabricate.

You are not here in this current incarnation to prove anything to anyone. The idea that you are not good enough or incapable is simply false. Everything you start is exactly that: a starting point. If the products you make do not measure up to the standards that others hold, those products are not "less than." In fact, they are "greater than" because you created them. In Thrifty Witchery, fabricating is not and never will be about selling the products you make. It is about tapping into your personal magick and bringing it out into the world to serve your needs.

It is common to see other people's crafts and compare yourself and the things you make to them. When you do this, you are setting yourself up for failure or disappointment. As is the case with every practice, it takes time to hone your fabricating skills. Your first product will not look as amazing as your tenth attempt. The goal is to keep trying, to persist in the face of your own demons. Shadow work and imposter syndrome can easily stand in your way if you let them. That is why it is called work. It is not meant to be easy. You must decide and believe that you are good enough, you are capable, and what you produce is just fine. We all have things we have made and feel proud of even though we know there may be someone who makes that same thing for a living and is better at crafting it than we are. Do not let perfect become the enemy of good.

How often do we compare ourselves to others and find ourselves somehow lacking? Being a witch does not insulate you from feeling envious or jealous of other people's possessions or accomplishments; after all, that is part of the human condition. A thing to keep in mind, though, is that pinning your focus and desires on other witches' tools in effect pins the focus of your spellcasting outside of your own intuition, wisdom, and intention.

We are not all master crafters. How could we be? When the darkest parts of yourself start telling you that you cannot do something you need to stand up to them. Look yourself in the mirror if you have to and say out loud: "Okay, I may not be the greatest, but this thing I am making is one hundred percent mine." Tell yourself, "I am empowered by the fact that I tried, and I will keep trying until this thing looks the way I want it to."

Here is an example. Like fabrication, writing is a craft. The first draft of this book was not publication ready. Even parts of the final draft were not publication ready at the time they were being written. We, and our crafting abilities, all wax and wane. Both of us have written some amazing paragraphs that have blown the other away. Frequently while writing this book, one of us has said to the other, "I just love this!" But there is another side to that coin—there have been some rotten paragraphs as well. Paragraphs where we have had to sit down with each other and say, "I don't get it. What are you saying here?" The creative process is hardly ever linear, yet somehow we all seem to reach the goal eventually if we just keep at it.

When fabricating a product or a tool, you are bound to have stumbling points. You will probably hit a roadblock and may feel as though you cannot move past it. It is in these moments that you take a break. Whether that break is for minutes, days, weeks, or months does not matter. For nearly two months while writing this book, Vincent did not write. He was stuck, lost in battle with his shadow when it whispered that maybe he is not enough. Martha stood by and gave him space, believing that this pause, however long it would be, would lead to something greater eventually. And she was right—it did.

Take a lesson from us: if you need to pause, do it. Be there for yourself. Do not beat yourself up because you are stalled in the fabrication process. When you are down, when you feel like what you are doing is pointless, lean into it. Give these moments their due attention. Once you work through that demon chewing at your ear, telling you lies about how imperfect you are, you too will emerge from your shadow and find that you have a rejuvenated approach that works for you.

Practical Practice
Letter Tile Power Words

Word formation games come with small tiles that each have a single letter on them, and these letter tiles can easily be repurposed for spellwork. This simple yet profound spell makes use of your intuition and is designed to activate your intention.

What You'll Need
> Letter tiles from a word formation game
> Piece of paper
> Writing implement

Numerology resource such as can be found on the
    internet
Flat surface to lay tiles on

What You'll Do

Lay the tiles facing up randomly on a flat surface. Close your
eyes and center yourself, taking three or more long slow
inhales through your nose and releasing your exhales through
your mouth. If possible, lay your hands lightly upon the tiles
and spread them around with a gentle motion. Bring the
question or goal you are seeking insight on to your awareness. Open your eyes and soften your focus as you look at
the letter tiles. Do not try to look for specific tiles to spell a
predetermined word; instead, try to see which letters catch
your particular attention and remove them from the rest of
the tiles. See what word(s) you can form from the letter tiles
that have caught your attention; these letters your intuition
has selected will give you insight about your question or goal.
Add up the numbers found on each individual tile; reduce any
multiple-digit numbers until you have a single-digit number.
The meanings associated with that number will provide additional insight around your query. If possible, keep the word(s)
on display either on your altar or someplace where you will
see it easily.

Example: Martha did this practice with "deadline" as her
stated goal; the word that resolved from the tiles was "write."
What does she need to do to meet her deadline? Write—nothing fancy or extra; just write. The numbers on the letter tiles
added to 8, a number relating to themes of abundance and/
or balance. If you want to use major arcana cards from the

tarot as a numerology resource, the number 8 corresponds to Strength in decks based on the Rider-Waite-Smith system.

Possible Uses
>Discernment
>Divination

PRACTICAL PRACTICE
Altars

Setting up an altar can be a crucial component of your witchcraft. Altars can be loud and proud or as subtle as a whispered incantation. No matter what your circumstances, visible or invisible, your altar functions as a central point of power for spellcrafting. A witch's altar can be literally anything they choose. From a matchbox to an extravagant table filled with statues, altars are personal and can be interpreted by each witch in various ways. An altar is a place of magick and a place where you do magick, one of the witch's energy centers, this is where your power coalesces to focus the endeavors you are manifesting. Whether it is dedicated to a deity, ancestors, or a specific spell, the altar is a place where witches harness their intentions and send them off into the world.

What You'll Need

Because altars are so personal, we are going to give you a few things to think about as you begin selecting items to construct your altar rather than listing supplies as in other fabrication projects.

Permanence

Deciding what the altar is made of or how it is contained should at least include a consideration of its functionality in support of your magick. An altar can be any table, shelf, flat top, or space used for a spiritual practice. It can be an elaborate dedicated space or hidden in plain sight, as visible as the coffee table in your living room. Your altars can be indoors or outside or both. If you need to set up and take down your altar frequently, think in terms of essentials so that you do not end up spending an inordinate amount of time setting out and storing your items.

Purpose

Will you primarily use your altar according to moon cycles? For seasonal rituals? Spellcasting? Think about how you plan to use your altar as you begin to collect items for it. For instance, are you planning to do some ancestor veneration? You can start with a picture or drawing of a deceased relative and access your intuition to build out your altar from that foundation. Or perhaps there is a particular animal or plant ally you have a connection with, and you have something that symbolizes it. Start with items that you already have a connection with, things that mean something special to you. They are perfect for your altar because they are representations of some of the truest parts of you.

Portability

Somewhat counter-intuitively, pocket altars offer tremendous set-up flexibility. They are often contained in small tin boxes that once held breath mints. You might think that such a tiny space would translate to a lot of restrictions, but the opposite can be true because you can pick up the pebbles, flowers, leaves, berries, feathers, and other things you find around you as you go through your day to add to your on-the-go altar. Add a small box of matches, a birthday candle, and a small vial of water and you will have every element represented.

Price

Money, or a lack of it, does not matter when it comes to magick. That is the whole point of this book. You do not need expensive accoutrements to feel power. Your intuition, wisdom, and intention are all it truly takes to get the results you want from spellcrafting. This holds true for your altar as well. If you are building an altar on a budget, stay within your means. You certainly should not forgo a meal just to buy a statue or special candle holder. In fact, the components you need to build an altar are probably already in your life. And if they are not, there are countless ways to find what you could use in inexpensive and thrifty ways, which we have covered in the chapters on foraging and finding.

What You'll Do

As you start to assemble the different components of your altar(s), you will be accessing the three cornerstones of your witchery: intuition, wisdom, and intention. Keep one thing in mind when building your altar: this is your space. This is the area in your environment where you will connect to whatever your Source is. This table, box, cabinet, or whatever it is was specifically meant for you and your magick, so it should only look the way you need it to. It should be as unique as you are and should be something that not only helps you feel empowered but also gives you deep satisfaction. As you sink into your intuition, wisdom, and intention and begin to fabricate your altar, you might keep the following or similar questions in mind:

Does this space feel sacred to you?
Do you feel your magick when you are stationed before it?
Have you built something you can take pride in?

Whether very small or rather large, your altar is your magickal center of the world, your omphalos, so you must feel and believe that it increases your power. It should make you feel happy and connected to your magick. With your intuition, wisdom, and intention as your guides, your altar can and should be as dynamic as you are. And just like you, it will develop and evolve over time.

Possible Uses
Ritual
Ancestor and / or deity veneration
Spellcasting
Esbat and sabbat celebrations

Fabricating Your Desires

Fabricating is all about the process: the manner in which you imbue your magick into what you make, what you deem necessary for your practice, and your self-identified strengths and weaknesses. In doing this, you will find that you are able to grow not only as a witch but as a creator as well. When you harness your own abilities and learn from the mistakes you make along the way, you grow.

Chances are, using your intuition was not easy the first time you started paying attention to it but it became easier the more you accessed it. Gaining wisdom is normally a slow and tedious process. Learning to direct your intentions is something you will likely work on for the rest of your witchy life. The first time you went foraging, you might not have known what to expect. And when you decided to search for a needed object, you may not have had the confidence that you would find it. Your skill in fabricating can be grown just like these other skills.

You will not be perfect the first time you fabricate anything. You will stall. You will put off projects. And you will beat yourself up over all sorts of things while making your tools. But when you make it through and see what you have produced, you are going to feel amazing. That amazing feeling might not be there the first time or the hundredth time, but it is coming. It will arrive. Again, fabrication is not just about making things, nor is it only about infusing your magick and yourself into an item that is all yours. It is also about persistence. So keep trying. Keep making. Be penny-wise and embrace your empowerment and the Thrifty Witch inside of you.

Witchcraft Is Not a Destination; It's a Journey

In the end, there are no hard and fast rules to magick; instead, there are guidelines and commonalities that can be found across individual practices and magickal systems. While this single book does not contain every possible truth that exists in witchcraft, it does contain some crucial essentials.

Magick resides in all things. There is an etheric power that each of us is able to tap into once we train ourselves to be sensitive to it. That power flows through everything from the kitchen table to the natural world to ourselves. When we seek a connection to that magick, we are can lean into the truth of our interconnectedness with all that is; we are one with each other, the world around us, and the Source that brings all things into existence.

Through intention, wisdom, and intuition, we are able to magickally navigate the world we live in. We can apply these skills to synthesize our understanding of magick into a singular, power-filled practice, and then use the power we gain through this understanding to manipulate our experiences into optimal outcomes that benefit us.

You are the primary tool for your magick—there is nothing else you absolutely need in order to manifest the desired outcome you are working toward. Use what is available to help you focus your power, but never lose sight of the truth that all that you need already resides within you—this is the heart of Thrifty Witchery. The confidence that you are enough is sufficient. Never falter in the sure knowledge that everything you need you already possess.

Your essence is as unique as a fingerprint; there is no one like you, and there is nothing like your magick. What your witchcraft looks like is not required to reflect anything but your truest self. Whether your craft is light, dark, or somewhere in between, remain true to yourself and not to the aesthetics popularized in social media. Your magick will look like *you*, and that is exactly how it should be.

You will always be finding your way. Witchcraft is not a destination, it is a journey. It does not matter if you are a crone, a middle-aged man, or a new witch just starting on their journey. There is nothing about your spellcraft set in stone. Your witchery will evolve and expand as you do. Give it room to become as powerful as you believe it to be. Remember that practice does not make you perfect—practice makes you powerful.

Particularly in the United States, the corporate-centric overculture we live in teaches us from a very young age that the world around us is a collection of things meant for consumption and commodification. This worldview gives value of our every interaction according to strictly transactional terms— "what do I get from it?" "What's in it for me?" We see, we take, we use, and after depleting a resource, we look for fresh resources to once again plunder to nothingness.

The consumer-focused worldview ought not be the witch's way. We are on the planet, and we are of the planet, and how we interact with the earth not only has a ripple effect on the rest of the ecosystem but also sends to every corporeal and incorporeal entity a crystal-clear message that tells them just what we think of them.

Thrifty Witchery offers us the opportunity to live in harmony with the energies surrounding us. It is a way that values and honors our relationships with air, fire, water, earth, and spirit in all their manifestations. This way of living does not define value in terms of how much we can buy or how on-trend our tools are, but instead in terms of the degree of authenticity existing in our relationships with ourselves and each element.

When you lean into your self-empowerment and intuition, wisdom, and intention, you quickly realize you are already enough because magick is in your DNA. You already have all the tools you need, and the tools you will forage, find, and fabricate will serve as focus objects uniquely tuned to your magickal signature.

Your power is your treasure, and no one can take it from you. Now go a-witchin' and a-wanderin' and see how far your magick will take you.

Acknowledgments

Ernest Hemmingway once said, "there is nothing to writing; all you do is sit down at a typewriter and bleed." Just like magick exacts a cost from those who would use it, so too did this book, which underwent a substantial rewrite from its birth as an idea to the text you now hold. Along the way, we wrangled with shaping a unique, identifiable magickal practice that is genuinely accessible to anyone regardless of income, physical ability, gender, or background.

While we share many ideas about how magick works, there were several points during the writing process when we realized both of us held some understandings that were profoundly different from the other person's gnosis. There were individual ideas we were passionate about including, and we were committed to doing so in a way that still honored the other person's magickal capital-T Truths. Because we kept perfect love and perfect trust—and the book—at the center of our writing partnership, in these instances we were able to forge our individually held beliefs into a dynamic amalgam that would honor both of our viewpoints and make sense while enriching our friendship and deepening our mutual respect for each other.

Like so many Pagan authors before us, we are so grateful for Jason Mankey and the door he opened for each of us several years ago at the Patheos blog site. Jason's commitment to the Pagan community includes encouraging new voices and giving them access to platforms that give them visibility for a wide audience. In doing so, he has helped to shape our community for years to come. We'd also like to thank our editor at Llewellyn, Heather Greene, for her insightful comments and continued commitment to the book. Our gratitude extends to everyone at Llewellyn who helped bring the final product to the bookshelves.

Martha

I want to especially thank my husband and soulmate, Tom, for his unwavering support of my witchery and unflagging belief in my ability to write this book. I also thank my sons, Aaron and Jacob, and my extended family for gracefully giving me the space to be who I am without feeling any judgmentalism or prejudice. As always, I'm grateful for my sister, Laura, gone too soon from this plane but ever-present in my heart.

Without Vincent, *Thrifty Witchery* would not have happened, and I'm so profoundly grateful to him for writing this book with me. It's no secret that my writing can occasionally be fairly abstruse, especially when it comes to the metaphysical components presented in this book. Vincent was never reluctant to tell me when I was too much up in my head ("too swords-y") in a way that managed to affirm and respect the philosophies I was laboring to articulate, which in turn allowed me to hear what he was saying without defensiveness. No egos were damaged in the making of this book!

Libraries are often rookeries for readers who will someday be writers, and I've been so lucky to have had ready access to an incredibly wide range of resources from a very young age. We should all be in awe of the work librarians do in support of their readers and their communities. In particular, I give a shout-out to the San Antonio Public Library's Landa branch. Some of my happiest childhood moments were spent in this lovely stucco and stone building, feeling the wooden floors creak around me as I soaked my soul in the sight, sound, and smell of books. In my college years, TCU's Mary Couts Burnett Library was full of mysterious yet-to-be discovered treasures, and my evenings working behind the desk and searching for lost books in the stacks were immensely satisfying. Finally, hats-off to the electronic lending programs that libraries such as those in Cedar Rapids, IA; Naperville, IL; and Miami, FL have in place—you saved my sanity these past several years.

And last, but in no way least, I'd like to thank the people who love me just the way I am and who have encouraged me to speak my Truths: Andrea Gufstason, Kelley Trombley-Freytag, Beth and Steve Jordan, Laura Ingersoll, H. Byron Ballard, Susana Morse, Traci Ardren, Cossette Paneque, Kristy Marquez, Joseph Zolobczuk, and the local Miami Pagan MeetUp group—you are all amazing!

Vincent

To my husband and sons, everything I do is for the three of you first and foremost. To my sister, thanks for telling me I was a witch before I even fully embraced it. To my extended family, thank you for believing in me even when it was hard to do. And to Martha, you are my writing lobster, and I will walk around any tank with my claw hooked to yours. I know I can be ridiculously direct. Thank you for understanding my communication language.

Bibliography

Baird, Benjamin, Anna Castenovo, Olivia Gosseries, Giulio Tononi. "Frequent lucid dreaming associated with increased functional connectivity between frontopolar cortex and temporoparietal association areas" in *Sci Rep* 8, 17798 (2018). https://doi.org/10.1038/s41598-018-36190-w.

Balthazar, Seth. "Abracadabra: 'As I Speak, I Create,'" Seth Balthazar website, April 18, 2021, https://sethbalthazar.com/2021/04/18/abracadabra-as-i-speak-i-create/.

Bel, Bekah Evie. "I'm An Armchair Pagan." *HearthWitch Down Under* (blog), *Patheos*, May 17, 2017, https://www.patheos.com/blogs/hearthWitchdownunder/2017/05/im-armchair-pagan.html.

Berry, Jennifer, and Alana Biggers. "Endorphins: Effects and how to increase levels," *Medical News Today*, February 6, 2018, https://www.medicalnewstoday.com/articles/320839.

Ciaccia, Chris. "Civil War-era 'Witch Bottle' Found in Virginia," Fox News, January 27, 2020, https://www.foxnews.com/science/civil-war-witch-bottle-found-virginia.

Dachis, Adam. "Instead of Saying 'I Don't Have Time' Say 'It's Not a Priority'," LifeHacker website, March 13, 2012, https://www.lifehacker.com/instead-of-saying-i-dont-have-time-say-its-not-a-pr-5892948.

Daley, Jason. "A Sorceress' Kit Was Discovered in the Ashes of Pompeii", *Smithsonian Magazine,* August 14, 2019, https://www

.smithsonianmag.com/smart-news/sorceresss-kit-was
-discovered-ashes-pompeii-180972907/.

Estrada, Jessica. "How Your Perception is Your Reality, According to Psychologists," Well + Good website, February 7, 2020, https://www.wellandgood.com/perception-is-reality/.

George, Alexandra L. "Oracles/Sibyls," King's College Oxford Women's History department website, February 9, 2007. https://departments.kings.edu/womens_history/ancoracles.html.

Gorham, Julia. "The Value of Play for Young Children," Montessori Rocks website, October 26, 2017, https://montessorirocks.org/value-of-play-for-young-children/.

Hallo, William W., and William Kelly Simpson. *The Ancient Near East: A History.* New York: Harcourt, Brace, Jovanovich, 1971.

Hanif, Muhammad Asif, Haq Nawaz, Muhammad Mumtaz Khan, Hugh J. Byrne, eds. "Bay Leaf," *Medicinal Plants of South Asia: Novel Sources for Drug Discovery.* (Amsterdam, NL: Elseveir, 2020), https://doi.org/10.1016/C2017-0-02046-3.

Hutton, Ronald. *The Triumph of the Moon: A History of Modern Pagan Witchcraft.* New York: Oxford University Press, 1999.

Kerr, Breena. "Tarot is Trending, and Dior Predicted This Months Ago," *New York Times*, October 25, 2017, https://www.nytimes.com/2017/10/25/style/tarot-cards-dior.html#~:text=Tarot%2Ddeck%20sales%20in%20general,director%20for%20U.S.%20Games%20Systems.

Lane, Megan. "Hoodoo Heritage: A Brief History of American Religion." Master's thesis, University of Georgia 2008, https://getd.libs.uga.edu/pdfs/lane_megan_e_200805_ma.pdf.

Lawrence, Paul and Nitin Nohria. *Driven: How Human Nature Shapes Our Choices*, (Hoboken, NJ: Jossey-Bass Publishing, 2002), as

quoted by Josh Kaufman in *The Personal MBA*. New York: Portfo-
lio/Penguin Random House 2020, https://personalmba.com
/core-human-drives/.

Laurens, Eli. "How to Use Crystals to Generate Energy," Sciencing
website, updated March 2018, https://sciencing.com/use
-crystals-generate-electricity-6729045.html.

Mack, Julie. "The 6 Bible verses on homosexuality, and differing interpretations," *Kalamazoo Gazette,* updated Jan 20 2019, https://
www.mlive.com/news/kalamazoo/2015/08/the_7_bible
_verses_on_homosexu.html.

Mankey, Jason. "Wicca: Misconceptions & Misidentity," *Raise the
Horns* (blog), February 2, 2021, https://www.patheos.com
/blogs/panmankey/2021/02/wicca-misconceptions
-misidentity/.

Mooney, Thorn. *The Witch's Path: Advancing Your Craft at Every Level*.
Woodbury, MN: Llewellyn Publications, 2021.

Nunez, Kirsten, and Elaine K. Nuo. "Lucid Dreaming: Controlling
the Storyline of Your Dreams," Healthline website, June 17,
2019, https://www.healthline.com/health/what-is-lucid
-dreaming, June 2019.

O'Sullivan, Joanne. *Book of Superstitious Stuff: Weird Happenings,
Wacky Rites, Frightening Fears, Mysterious Myths & Other Bizarre
Beliefs*. Watertown, MA: Charlesbridge Publishing, 2010.

Place, Robert M. "A History of Oracle Cards," Tarot & Divination
Decks with Robert M. Place website, October 25, 2015, https://
robertmplacetarot.com/2015/10/25/a-history-of-oracle-cards/.

Quinion, Michael. "Abracadbra," Worldwide Words website, updated
December 19, 2005, https://www.worldwidewords.org/qa
/qa-abr1.htm.

Regur, Aimee. "Witch Hazel: Hamamelis Virginiana," Pangea Organics website, February 28, 2017, https://pangeaorganics.com/blogs/pangea-blog/witch-hazel-hamamelis-virginiana?_pos=1&_sid=3b6ca7abc&_ss=r.

Rosenbriar, Meg, and Louisa Dean. "Witch With Me Census 2020," Witch with Me website, https://witchwithme.com/witch-with-me-census-2020-2/.

Saunders, David T., Chris A. Roe, Graham Smith, Helen Clegg. "Lucid dreaming incidence: A quality effects meta-analysis of 50 years of research," *Consciousness and Cognition* 43 (June 2016): 197–215. DOI: https://doi.org/10.1016/j.concog.2016.06.002

Scott, Michael. *Delphi: A History of the Center of the Ancient World*. Princeton, NJ: Princeton University Press, 2014.

Silver, Sandra Sweeny. "Casting Lots in the Bible," Early Church History website, (no date), https://earlychurchhistory.org/beliefs-2/casting-lots-in-the-bible/.

Staff writers. "Dodona," Ancient Greece website, (no date), https://ancient-greece.org/history/dodona.html.

Staff writers. "The Legend of the Horseshoe," Kentucky Derby Museum website, March 11, 2014, https://www.derbymuseum.org/Blog/Article/52/The-Legend-of-the-Horseshoe.

Staff writers. "History at Home: Laurel Wreath Activity," Leonia Public Library, (no date), https://static1.squarespace.com/static/59fc7cafbff200c34f972a81/t/5e95dbb710c89d708989fd72/1586879418672/LaurelWreathActivity.pdf.

Staff writers. "The Water in You: Water and the Human Body," United States Geological Survey (USGS) Water Science School website, May 22, 2019, https://www.usgs.gov/special-topic

/water-science-school/science/water-you-water-and-human
-body?qt-science_center_objects=0#qt-science_center_objects.

Swift, Kaeli. "FAQs About Crows," Corvid Research website, (no
date), https://corvidresearch.blog/faqs-about-crows/.

Taylor, Astrea. *Intuitive Witchcraft: How to Use Intuition to Elevate Your
Craft.* Woodbury, MN: Llewellyn Publications, 2021.

Weinstein, Marion. *Personal Magic: A Modern-Day Book of Shadows for
Positive Witches.* Newburyport, MA: Weiser Books 2021.

Wen, Benebell. *Holistic Tarot: An Integrative Approach to Using Tarot for
Personal Growth.* Berkeley, CA: North Atlantic Books, 2015.

Woodcock, Victoria. "Why Tarot is Trending Again," *The Financial
Times,* April 16, 2021, https://www.ft.com/content
/c4afbc05-a715-4b83-9323-44e4c4f95ca5

To Write to the Authors

If you wish to contact the authors or would like more information about this book, please write to the author in care of Llewellyn Worldwide Ltd. and we will forward your request. Both the authors and publisher appreciate hearing from you and learning of your enjoyment of this book and how it has helped you. Llewellyn Worldwide Ltd. cannot guarantee that every letter written to the author can be answered, but all will be forwarded. Please write to:

Martha Kirby Capo and/or Vincent Higginbotham
% Llewellyn Worldwide
2143 Wooddale Drive
Woodbury, MN 55125-2989

Please enclose a self-addressed stamped envelope for reply,
or $1.00 to cover costs. If outside the U.S.A., enclose
an international postal reply coupon.

Many of Llewellyn's authors have websites with additional information and resources. For more information, please visit our website at http://www.llewellyn.com.